The Shoemaker

or

The Burning Flag of Tyranny

The story of a Jewish boy born in Russia in 1888 and how he came to the United States as a shoemaker in 1911.
The Biography of Louis Kerbel as told to

Joe L. Todd

NEW FORUMS

NEW FORUMS PRESS INC.

Published in the United States of America
by New Forums Press, Inc.1018 S. Lewis St.
Stillwater, OK 74074
www.newforums.com

Library of Congress Cataloging-in-Publication Data Pending

This book may be ordered in bulk quantities at discount from New
Forums Press, Inc., P.O. Box 876, Stillwater, OK 74076 [Federal I.D. No.
73 1123239]. Printed in the United States of America.

ISBN 10: 1-58107-351-8
ISBN 13: 978-1-58107-351-5

Table of Contents

Foreword

I was working for the Oklahoma Historical Society when I met Shifra Silberman in 1985. She told me her step grandfather, Louis Kerbel, lived in Tulsa and was in the Zionist movement in Russia and that I should visit him.

In a few weeks, she came to see me and said that her grandfather had fallen and broken his hip and was in the hospital in Tulsa and I should go before he passes. She gave me the hospital and room number and I took my audio recorder to the hospital and introduced myself. I asked if I could ask him a few questions and record him and he agreed. He answered every question and he talked about the Jewish Self Defense League in Czarist Russia. His story was phenomenal and I thought too good to be true.

At the library and found a Russian history book and a photograph of some of the Self Defense League members. I xeroxed the photo, removed the cut line and took it to Mr. Kerbel. He identified every person in the photo and I knew I had found a gold mine.

He left the hospital and I went to his apartment on a regular basis and completed about six hours of video tape over the next few years. His memory was extraordinary and it seemed he remembered every detail. He talked about his childhood in the Ukraine and being a shoemaker. He continued about the devastation of leaving his home and moving to Odessa on the Black Sea. He talked about how he came to the United States in 1911 and making his life here.

On one visit, I met the rabbi and as I was leaving, he walked out with me and told me that I had saved Mr. Kerbel's life. I asked how and he said when Mr. Kerbel broke his hip and was in the hospital, he had nothing to live for. He and his wife had no children and he was very depressed and his doctor said he is going downhill. The rabbi said,

"You appeared, showed an interest in his story, and you brought him out of his depression."

Mr. Kerbel was always upbeat and always in a good mood. Every time I went to visit him and asked how he was doing, he would always say, "I feel fine."

I went to visit him in the hospital right after his 100th birthday in December 1988. As I walked into the room and asked how he was doing. He said, "I feel fine." I got a call that afternoon and was informed he had passed away just a few hours after I left. I was honored to be a pall bearer at his funeral.

I cannot say enough about Mr. Kerbel. One thing I will always remember, is that he would always cry and say," I came to this country with seventy-five cents in my pocket and now I am wealthy and I owe everything to this country and will give everything back."

Mr. Kerbel is one of the most fascinating if not the most fascinating person I have ever met. When I asked if he was bitter about his family dying in the Holocaust, he said he would like to think he was a better man than to be bitter. This was Mr. Kerbel.

Joe L. Todd

Chapter One
A Jewish Family in Russia

There was a nice glow from the oven the night I was born. This is what my mother told me. That was on the 15th of December in the Christian year 1888 in the village of Roshen. Roshen was in the Ukraine and the family had lived there for generations. The temperature was 30 degrees below zero as I have been told. My father was Abraham

This is a photograph of Mama and Papa.

Simonevich Kerbel, the shoemaker of Roshen. My mother was Lebaugh Shmukler Kerbel from the village of Rovno.

I was named Louis Abrahamevich Kerbel. In Russia the middle name of each son was the first name of the father. My brother, born three and a half years after me was Solomon Abrahamevich Kerbel and the next was named Moses Abrahamevich Kerbel. The last was named Simon Abrahamevich Kerbel. The names of the daughters didn't seem to matter, but they were named Gueti and Rosa.

I was the first-born. Mama told me the story of how the village midwife brought two women with her since I was

This is a photograph of Mama with Gueti and Rosa.

Mama's first child. As the three women attended Mama, Papa had several men from the village to celebrate the birth of his first son. Papa always knew I was going to be a son and not a daughter. Sons were much more important than daughters, in those days anyway.

When a good fire was going, the house was warm and made everyone feel secure. There was such a fire the day I was born. The women cleaned up and I was passed from woman to woman and then to Papa. One man brought vodka and Papa joined in the toast. Papa didn't drink, but the birth of a son was a special occasion. We were Orthodox Jews and Papa followed the law. Mama's sister had come from Rovno to take over the household chores. The village women offered to take over the chores, but being orthodox, Papa thanked them very nicely and refused. The whole village knew why my aunt was here and she was accepted. When she was not cooking or cleaning, she was talking to the village women about the world outside of Roshen.

Our house looked similar to this but there are no photos of our house in Roshen.

The street in Roshen ran north and south and our house was near the center of town on the west side of the street and faced east. It only had one room about 30 feet square and was made of logs with a packed dirt floor. I helped Papa build houses like ours when I was old enough to work with him. The bark was stripped from the logs and then stacked. The logs were tapered, so each succeeding log had to be reversed to keep the wall level. Moss that grew on trees was used as chinking between the logs. This moss continued to grow between the logs and formed a tight seal for the walls. One long tree was cut for the ridge beam then other logs were notched and used as rafters. Smaller trees were cut and placed across the rafters and then covered with wheat straw. We even had thermal pane windows. A pane of glass was on the outside and a pane on the inside. The dead air space between was good insulation against the Russian winter. Those glass panes were very difficult to acquire and also very expensive. Every family protected those glass panes because if one was broken, a replace-

This is what an oven in the homes looked like. This one is similar to the one in our home.

ment came from Kiev and would take weeks. The glass was never a standard size and a frame had to be made to fit the glass. The glass pane never fit the frame in the wall. The furnishings in our house were meager, whatever Papa made. A few chairs, a table for eating and another table for food preparation and Papa made two cabinets for the dishes. We had two beds, one for Mama and Papa and the other for the children. The oven was right in the middle of the room. It was about six feet square and made of clay blocks about six inches thick. Winters in the Ukraine can be merciless, but the people learned to adjust.

Roshen had one street where 25 families lived. The

This is a photo of a Russian village that looks like Roshen. As far as I know, no photographs were ever taken of Roshen. Courtesy Johnstown Area Heritage Association.

houses were on both sides of the street and were about 40 to 50 feet apart. The out buildings were behind each house. We were the only Jewish family in Roshen. Life was simple then, you were born, followed in your father's footsteps then died, all in the same village. Life hadn't changed in the Ukraine for generations.

Neighbors helped each other in those days. Even though we were Jews, we were part of the community. When a couple married, the whole town joined to build their house. This is how I learned to build the log houses. Our house was made of logs, but there were also houses made of mud. The men gathered dirt, rocks and straw on the house site. The floor plan of the house was laid out then water was poured on the ingredients to make a thick mud, and the men began raising the walls. The mud was thick enough that it stood by itself without a form. The mud walls were

This is how the logs were joined at the corners in the houses with the moss between the logs and this kept our house warm.

12 to 14 inches thick. Wooden forms were inserted for the windows then the double panes of glass were inserted. Just as with our house, trees were cut for the ridge beam and rafters and wheat straw formed the thatch roof.

The village was well organized. On the north end of the street was the church that had a school attached, which was also made of logs. I attended that school for only two years. Being the only Jews, there wasn't a Synagogue for us. I had never seen a Synagogue, even though Papa told stories of attending the one in Kiev. The school had one nun who always dressed in black and cared for the church and was the teacher in the one-room school. She taught all the boys in Roshen and the surrounding farms in the school. The head of the town was the mayor appointed by the Czar. I doubt if Nicholas actually appointed the mayor, and probably some minor official in Minsk had that job. The mayor was also the overseer and tax collector. Being the tax collector, he had the nicest house and his family wore the best clothes in town. The job of mayor was hereditary and had been in his family for several generations. The mayor also appointed the priest at the church, therefore he had complete authority over the village. I had been inside the church on many occasions and there was a chair reserved for the Czar. I marveled at the icons on the wall and even sat in the Czar's chair one time. I was told this chair for the Czar would be found in any Orthodox Church in Russia. The Czar was head of the church but he never came to our village. The Mayor reported to the government in Minsk who reported to Moscow.

The one street in Roshen was wide enough to make a "U" turn with a wagon and team of horses. It was good planning by the men who founded the village. Roshen was an old farming village and Papa told me it dated back to the time of Peter the Great. Behind the houses were the gardens, barns and outhouses. Great care was taken to build the out buildings close to the house due to the winters. Temperatures of forty- and fifty-below zero were not uncommon and the winds were horrible. Snow would be six or seven feet deep and lasted for months. A path was kept open between the house and the barn and outhouses. These structures were about fifteen feet apart. The snow drifted up against the barn and we kept a small fire inside all winter long. The insulation from the snow and the fire kept the animals warm. We kept a fire in the large oven in the house and that kept us warm. During the winter, we brought the chickens inside the house and they stayed under the oven. Nothing could survive outside in the Russian winter

I can barely remember when Solomon was born. He was the second in the family. I was almost three and a half years old. I remember that night because it was different. The house was filled with people, the women were busy and the men were toasting. Mama had not been able to hold me as she normally did and the village women cleaned and kept me company. Mama cooked until her sister came from Rovno again to take over the household chores. That was Papa's rule. Papa told me I could go out and play with the other boys in the village. I always enjoyed playing with the other boys but this was late in the afternoon and was unusual. Suddenly there was someone new in the house. I had seen many children born in Roshen, but this was different, it was in my house. I had a baby brother named Solomon and Mama helped me adjust. I always seemed to adjust to the situation. I wondered if Solomon would survive because many children died in infancy in the village and the cemetery was filled with their tombstones but Solomon did survive.

I think all the families in Roshen were farmers except us and we were the shoemakers. Wheat was the main crop. The Ukraine was the breadbasket of Russia and most of the wheat consumed in Europe came from the farms in our area. Every farm had animals and one man cared for the cattle, one cared for the horses and one cared for the sheep. Each morning the three men would gather together the animals in their care and take them to the fields to graze then bring them back in the evening before dark. The cattle always knew where they belonged. The barns always had the door open and the cattleman would follow the cattle to their respective barns, but the men with the horses and sheep had to lead their animals to the barns. The barn doors were then closed and locked. All the barns had to be locked because of bears and wolves that roamed the countryside back then. People talk about horse sense, but I think cattle have much more sense than horses. Several families raised hogs, but they never left their pen and Papa instructed all of us that the hogs were unclean and we were to have nothing to do with them. Everyone in Roshen knew we were Jews and we were part of the village as everyone was and this was the way it had been for generations. If a family needed something, the village provided it. Many times Mama and Papa went to help a family and he always told us that if we needed help, the village would be there for us.

Papa was the town cobbler. As was the custom, the sons followed in the steps of the father. Papa was a shoemaker, so I became a shoemaker. If a family was rich, they could send their sons off to study another profession. There was only one rich family in the town and of course that was the mayor. Everyone else was poor but we all helped each other. No one went hungry and if a mother or father died, the village all helped that family. I can't remember when Papa began instructing me in the art of the shoemaker as his Papa had done to him and every father to his son in our family. Papa took great care to instruct me in the proper method of making a quality boot and shoe. My first training was in the proper care of the tools. They had to be sharpened, cleaned and oiled daily. The tools were expensive and Papa made sure I respected and took care of them. Most of the tools had belonged to my Grandfather Simon.

I was then taught the different types of leather. Certain leather was used to make shoes and other types were used to make boots and it was a necessity to know which was which. Leather was expensive and nothing was wasted. I was taught how to fashion the shoe or boot and to stitch the pieces together. I learned to stitch small leather pieces together that were too small for a boot or shoe. Each stitch had to be just right. He ripped out many stitches in those early years and I restitched until Papa thought I was good enough to make a Kerbel shoe. I do remember that my stitching lessons went hand in hand with my Hebrew lessons from Papa. Papa had the foot molds and I took great pains to copy Papa in how to measure the foot to make a good fitting shoe. In the final shoe, Papa did all the stitching and I made the bottom of the boot and shoe. Papa always insisted the stitching had to be just right. Because of this I became more proficient in making the bottoms.

It was many years before I was allowed to make a pair of shoes for a customer. My first customer was Mrs. Kerowski. She was an old widow in the village that everyone loved. She knew the history of every family in the village and always had a smile and happy greeting for everyone. Papa watched as I measured each foot and he wrote down the measurements as I recited them. They were my first pair of shoes that I made without Papa's help and I took extra special care. They were button shoes with a small heel. I was proud of those shoes and Papa was beaming when she picked them up. I fitted them on her and they did look nice. She walked in them and she said they were the most comfortable shoes she had ever had on her feet. Years later I saw her son and he said he had to tell me something. He explained that one shoe hurt in one spot, but she would never dream of telling me. She knew they were my first pair of shoes and were very important to me. She brought her old shoes in to be repaired. Papa offered to do the work, but she refused. She said that since I was such a good shoemaker, I would repair all of her shoes. She also said she was saving that first pair of shoes for church where everyone could see them. She wore those shoes every Sunday and told everyone the care I took in making them. I often think of her, how a grand lady she was to wear those shoes with that one spot hurting her foot, but she made a small boy and his father very proud.

The daily routine in Roshen never changed. Maybe a bear or wolf would wander through the village at night, or a roof would catch fire and then there were the births and the deaths. The cemetery was on the road north out of town and it was always very well kept. Great respect was given to those who had lived in the village before us. Every day was about the same, the seasons changed, and the people got older. The village celebrated Christmas and Easter and we celebrated Hanukkah and Passover and we all celebrated the birthday of the Czar. We may have been Jews but we were good Russians. I watched the other people celebrate and sometimes I wished that I could celebrate their holidays and they could celebrate ours.

One thing I do remember was watching the sun rise each morning. It would slowly come over the hills and I would watch the sunlight play through trees on the hills and how the shadows it made. I didn't think much of it then but it was amazing to watch that sun rise every morning. I would then watch the sun set behind the hills on the west of Roshen and how the shadows would lengthen. As I grew I noticed how the sun moved through the sky. It headed north in spring and summer and then back south in fall and winter.

We had a town watchman that patrolled the streets at night and kept a lookout for the bears and wolves. The bears never came in the winter because they hibernated and the wolves never came in the summer. I remember one bear that did come in the winter and everyone was terrified. I was about seven years old and Papa told us to stay inside the house. He said a bear never comes in the winter unless something is wrong. Turned out he was rabid and the men killed it but I was never told how. The wolves were always found in the forest from spring to fall and they would wander through once in a while in the wintertime. If they were not bothered, they roamed on through. It was very important that nothing was left outside to attract the forest animals. The watchman carried a long pole with a sharpened point. This was used to fend off the wolves if necessary. He was good with that pole and if he needed help, he would ring a small bell he carried. If he ever rang that bell, the whole village would come out. The only time I remember him sounding the alarm was the bear in the wintertime.

One day Papa went to Rovno to buy leather for boots. The trip took two days, but Rovno had the nearest store. We didn't have a store in Roshen, the town was not large enough. Papa made the trip once a month and always took a man from the village with him. On this trip, Papa was going alone. It was spring and all the men in the village were busy in the fields. He promised he would not travel at night and would be on guard for highwaymen at all times. Papa was a big man and would have no problem defending himself, even though he had never carried a weapon in his life. He said his good byes and told us he would return in two days. While he was gone, I worked on a pair of shoes and Solomon kept me company in the shop. Papa had been instructing him in the proper use of caring for tools and the various types of leather just as he had done with me. Mama was sweeping the dirt floor of the house and Gueti and Rosa were sewing a new dress for Mama and a new shirt for Papa. They were old enough to take over the task of making the clothes for the family. Mama had taught them well. She instructed Gueti and Rosa how to care for the needle and thread as well as Papa had instructed me in the care of the leather tools. After they made the dress and shirt, they were to make new shirts for us boys in preparation for the Rabbi's next visit.

The sun was setting and Mr. Serakoff brought the sheep to the barn behind our house. The cow was already home. Mama walked outside with me and we greeted Mr. Serakoff. He was a friendly old man in his seventies. He had known my grandfather Shmukler and often told stories about him in Rovno. Mr. Serakoff had traveled quite a bit. He had been to Kiev many times and even been to Moscow and St. Petersburg. I listened to his stories of grandfather and the places he had traveled and I knew one day I would also travel. I wanted to see Moscow and St. Petersburg. My mother told me her brother, Herman had moved to America before I was born. To be more American, he changed his name from Shmukler to Golden and lived in a city named Dallas. I had never been out of the area around Roshen. I wanted to see Rovno, Moscow, St. Petersburg and Dallas. I wanted to see what was on the other side of those hills around Roshen.

I grew up with the other boys in Roshen and knew their parents because Papa made shoes and boots for everyone in the village as his father before him. The only fights in the village were among the boys in the school and that was normal the world over. They really weren't fights, more like skirmishes. Looking back through the eyes of a child, those were the best years of my life. Mama and Papa were friendly to everyone and in return everyone was friendly to them. I knew of no bad feelings toward anyone. Life was good then.

Two village women came along and they talked with Mama for a few minutes. The sun had set and we went inside and Rosa was preparing the pine knots for the evening. We couldn't afford candles and for light we burned pine knots. The knots were full of rosin and burned bright enough to give a good light. One of my jobs was to gather the knots in the forest. Roshen was on the edge of the

Black Forest of the Ukraine. We finished supper and Mama mended a pair of Papa's socks. Solomon and I were cleaning and oiling the tools for the next day. The scarf outlined Mama's face as she worked on the sock and the fire from the knot made shadows that played on her features. Mama never removed that scarf covering her head in the daytime and she always ensured her head was covered as well as Gueti and Rosa when they left the house, as did most of the women in the village. The only time it was removed was bedtime. She was a good wife and mother.

Clothes were washed almost everyday to make sure the family was properly dressed. Each morning she had the clothes laid out for the day and she collected the previous days clothes. They were checked for holes that had to be mended. Repairs were made and then laundered. The laundry was done by hand in the stream that was about 500 feet from our house. Mama made our soap separate from the other village women because of the fat used, but all the women did the laundry together. The stream was also the water supply for the village and had to be protected. All washing was done downstream from the village and all privies were placed so as not to contaminate the water. The other women made their soap from the lard rendered from the hogs but Mama used fat from the beef. I'm not sure if it made as good soap as the hog fat, but the hog was unclean. I had never seen Mama make soap and she didn't render fat and I don't know where our soap came from. All I know is that we didn't use soap made from hog fat.

Another job I had was to make sure there was enough wood for the oven. The oven heated the house, and Mama cooked in it. As another part of our daily chores, Solomon and I fed two cows and six sheep and made sure the barn door was secure against bears and wolves. Moses was old enough to work around the shop, but not with the animals. We always went to the barn the same time each day. This was the time the girls and Mama prepared for bed.

Mama was up early. It was strange not to have Papa in the house, his large frame silhouetted by the early light filtering through the window. Being the oldest, I was in charge while Papa was gone. I felt very strange that I should be in charge of Mama, that was tradition, but Mama was really in charge, I was just a small boy and she was a wise, married woman. After breakfast, I began working on a pair of boots for Mr. Serakoff. He came for the sheep and Leonoid came for the cow. I watched as they walked down the street with the village herds following them. The forest loomed in the direction they were walking. I had climbed to the top of many of the hills and there was always another hill in the distance. I wondered what was on the other side of those hills. Someday I would climb those hills and see what was over there. Clouds were gathering on the hills and the days were growing shorter. Before long winds of the Russian winter would fill the streets as it had for generations. Man fought the Russian winter but never won. All we could do was adapt and hope the approaching snows would be merciful.

The two days Papa was gone passed quickly. Mama gave an audible sigh of relief when he returned. She was always nervous when Papa was gone, even though there was nothing to fear in Roshen. Solomon and I helped bring in the bundles of leather. On top were the pieces of leather Papa had selected by hand for Mama's shoes. He took special care in choosing the leather for her shoes. Papa was never one to show emotion. He greeted Mama, gave her his standard kiss on the forehead and then greeted us children. From the pocket of his coat he took out a small leather pouch and handed it to Mama. It was a gift. Papa said business had been good and she deserved a gift. Mama's eyes were beaming. Gifts were rare and she was full of anticipation. She took great care in unwrapping the treasure. It was wrapped in leather because it was cheaper than paper. Paper was reserved for special letters to special people and being in the shoe business, leather was plentiful. It was unwrapped and she held it up for all of us to see. It was made of clay, about three inches in diameter and two inches tall with a small hole in the top. A piece of twine stuck out of the hole. I looked at it in wonder, having no idea what it was. Papa took another pouch from his pocket and unwrapped it. It was a bottle. He took the item from Mama and poured a liquid into the hole. He then set it on the table and took a twig from the oven and lit the twine. It was an oil lamp. I had never seen one. It burned with a brightness I had never seen before. I had never seen such a thing. I was amazed at the shadows it cast on the walls. We all stood and stared at it.

Word of the lamp spread through the village. It was the first one in the village and everyone had to come see it. Papa stood proudly by the door as the people came and went. Mama, as with tradition, sat next to the lamp sewing. The women stood next to her and talked about how proud she must be to have such a gift. Mama was proud, but she never boasted. It was not proper. We had something new in the village and no one else had one. Mama protected that lamp and the bottle of oil. She was the only one that could fill the lamp. She even told Papa to leave her lamp alone. I think that was the only time Mama told Papa to do something and he obeyed. She would have been heart-

Mama's oil lamp.

broken if something happened to that lamp. After the village came to see the lamp, Papa settled in and lit his pipe. Papa always smoked his pipe at night. That was the only luxury he gave himself. He raised his own tobacco in our garden. I never knew if Mama approved of his pipe or not. If she disapproved, she kept it to herself. In those days, the women never went against their husband.

During the holidays we exchanged gifts. Solomon and I made a Menorah out of clay. We tried to bake it in the oven, but it wasn't up to our expectations. Papa admired it and said it was more valuable than gold and fitted the first candle for Hanukkah in our Menorah. I couldn't understand Papa, because who wouldn't want a Menorah made of gold. Just think of the places you could travel and the fine horses you could buy if you had a gold Menorah. Moses was young, but he was good at carving with his knife. He made small trinkets for each family member. Papa bought a small bag of marbles for Solomon and a new leather knife for me. He bought material for new dresses for the girls. For Mama he bought a small-framed photograph of the Czar and Czarina. Mama hung it in a prominent place for all to see. We exchanged these gifts during Hanukkah.

The Rabbi tried to visit Roshen once a month to celebrate the Sabbath. There were three other Jewish families that lived within a three-day journey from Roshen. Our house was about in the center where the four families lived so the other families always came to our house. The Kirchkoff's lived about 30 miles south of Roshen. The Kneidlik family lived 20 miles east of us and the Klaffki's lived 25 miles north of Roshen. Rabbi Kautzman always arrived before sundown on Friday. The Sabbath the Rabbi came was always was special. Papa ensured we observed the Sabbath, but the gathering with the Rabbi was always special. Mama and the girls cooked and cleaned, because everything had to be in order. She used to say how Mrs. Kirchkoff was a busy body and checked to see how clean the house was. Even the village joined in our anticipation. Anyone from the outside was welcome. Not that Roshen was isolated, people just didn't travel. Twenty miles was a long journey. The three families always arrived just before the Rabbi. Mama had a good meal fixed, and we all ate a hearty portion. This meal was special. Mama could not cook on the Sabbath. We could not perform any work during this period. Papa ensured the laws were obeyed. I can remember a few times when Mama or one of us kids was sick, then one did not have to obey the law of fasting. Everything had to be prepared for because no work could be performed on the Sabbath.

Igor Kirchkoff was just a year younger than I was and I always anticipated his arrival. We had become good friends, even though we saw each other about once a month. As soon as he arrived, he and I had to prepare the animals for the Sabbath. We went to the barn to put out enough feed and water that would last the whole day. We could not perform any chores or work on the Sabbath. We were to reflect on our heritage on that day. Igor and I were so busy talking and playing with the other boys our age, and it was difficult to reflect on "our heritage." Rosa told me the same thing years later. She and Gueti were so excited to have the girls at the house, Mama had trouble keeping them in line. I think Papa frowned on the frivolity of his children, but he never said anything. He did ensure no work or chores were performed.

Rabbi Kautzman spoke Russian, Hebrew, Yiddish, and German. I had never met a person that spoke so many different languages. Our house was turned into a Synagogue and on the Sabbath everyone gathered at our home. Igor, Solomon and me had to sit with the women behind the curtain that was hung across the room. The Rabbi had his Torah and his Hebrew was so much better than mine, but I was learning. I do recall that this Sabbath Papa had his special Yarmulke.

At bedtime, people slept everywhere. In the three families, there were nineteen people plus the Rabbi. They had to stay, we were not allowed to travel on the Sabbath. Mama pulled out blankets and made pallets on the floor. Of course bedding was brought with the families. Mama and Papa slept in their bed and the other bed was given to the Rabbi. All the boys slept in the barn. We piled straw into a big pile, and then put old blankets on top and mashed down the straw until it was comfortable. This was all accomplished before sundown. After going to bed, we talked long into the wee hours of the morning until one by one we fell asleep.

All the next day, Mama talked to the women about the world outside of Roshen. Who had married, who had children and who had died since their last visit. There was very little communication in those days. Our house became the synagogue. A curtain was strung across the room. The men were with the Rabbi in front of the curtain. The women, girls and boys under twelve years of age were behind the curtain. I had not had my Bar Mitzvah, so I sat with Igor and the women. Leonoid Kirchkoff always made sure that I knew he was thirteen and was able to sit with the men. I was only nine years old but I longed for the day I would be able to sit with the men. The Rabbi brought out the Torah and Papa always relished the chance to read from this copy. Papa had his own pointer that had belonged to his grandfather.

The Sabbath never lasted long enough. It was one of the few times people from outside our village came to Roshen. Sunday morning was the time for them to leave. It was dangerous to travel at night. They spent two nights with us and always left on Sunday morning. The three families knew most of the villagers in Roshen and always greeted each other as the Jews were leaving and the Christians were going to church. All the villagers were happy to see someone outside of Roshen. We respected each other. The

Christians had no problem with us and we had no problem with them, except when I went to school.

I was enrolled in the village school when I was seven years old. It was the only school in the area and of course was connected with the Orthodox Church. The schoolroom was about 20 by 40 feet and had benches made of rough-cut lumber. I think I told you there was one nun that taught in the school and took care of the church. Papa had given me a slate for my classes. He said education was very important and told me I would attend even if it was a Christian School. During the first week of classes, I asked the sister if I could see the inside of the church. I had known her for years and she said, of course. She took me inside and it was wonderful. I was fascinated by the paintings. The building was made of logs and had benches for the people. The first thing I noticed, there was no curtain separating the room as in our home. I was allowed to walk up to the altar where the priest gave his sermons. It was not made of rough-cut lumber as the benches, but was highly polished wood. She looked around and then told me I could sit in the chair reserved for the Czar. I sat down and looked around nervously. If I was caught sitting in the Czar's chair, what would happen. I only remained there a few seconds and left the church. I felt kind of strange, a Jew inside a church. I remember going home and asking Papa if the synagogues have a chair reserved for the Czar. He said if the Czar came to our synagogue, there would be a chair reserved for him. He then asked how I liked the inside of the church. I knew I was in trouble. He said it was good to see the church, but to remember that I was Jew.

Our classes consisted of mathematics, science, Russian and church lessons. Papa explained to me that the church lessons were good because they talked of God and that he had studied the Christian faith. He had done this so he would have a knowledge of it and be able to carry on good conversations. Papa said it was always good to know what one is talking about, and since we were the only Jews, most religious conversations were about the Christian faith. Papa also said we have the same God and the Christians came from our faith.

As each boy entered the schoolroom, he genuflected and crossed himself. They did this in front of an icon of Jesus in the room. I was the only one that did not do this, being a Jew. The sister said it was not necessary for me to genuflect, not being a Christian. She explained this to the other boys. Everyone in the room knew I was a Jew and knew we did not genuflect. It was not a problem that first year, but the second year was a different story. I don't know what started the problem, but a few of the boys started making comments that "the Christ killer does not cross himself." I tried to ignore the comments. Papa told me to just walk away from the troublemakers. There were only one or two making the comments. Everyone else thought nothing of the fact that I did not genuflect.

The comments continued and Papa warned me not to start trouble. He said he was not raising his sons to be troublemakers. One boy named Michael kept calling me "the Christ killer." I told him Christ was killed 1900 years ago and I was only eight years old. That didn't do any good. One morning Michael met me at the door and he had two other boys with him. The sister was not in the room yet. He said I was going to genuflect or else. I said I did not have to and was not going to do it. He threatened me and I turned to walk away when he pushed me from behind and knocked me down. I tried to defend myself but there were three of them. I was big for my age, but not with three attackers. They bloodied my nose and I was getting up when the sister arrived. She was furious and demanded to know who had done this. I glanced at Michael and he was sitting very still as were the other two. I didn't say anything. I was sent home and as I walked away I heard her raise her voice to the class of how disgusting violence was in any form and she was ashamed of the class. When I arrived home, Mama was horrified at the blood. The bleeding had stopped and she was wiping my face when there was a knock at the door. It was the Sister. She asked if I was all right. My nose was a little crooked and she said it was broken. She repeated that she was shocked at what happened and reprimanded the class. She apologized to Mama and told me she would ensure it didn't happen again. When she left, Mama asked me if I had done anything to cause this. I told her I hadn't. She asked if I had said or done anything to make the boys jealous. I realized then that we lived in a nicer house and Papa had a better income than their fathers and I made sure they knew this. I also made sure they knew we had the first oil lamp in the village. I think Mama knew that I made Michael and Alexis jealous, but she didn't say anything.

I told Papa I didn't want to go back to school again. He sat me down and asked why I felt this way. I said since I was a Jew I was not going to cross myself and it would only be a matter of time until I was in trouble again. He and Mama discussed the situation. They realized it was only a matter of time until it happened again. Mama also mentioned the comments I had made about our house and the oil lamp. I was always outgoing and there would be trouble again. I did not have to go back to school. I had mixed emotions about quitting because I enjoyed learning. Outside of school, Michael and Alexis and I had been friends. We had no trouble except for the normal boyhood squabbles. It took several weeks for the resentment and the bruises to go away. Papa knew it was best to remove the bone of contention. I also thought that he was afraid I might become accustomed to the Christian ceremonies.

The winter winds were approaching. The fleece on the sheep was thick and the cow had her winter coat. We cut wood for the oven, checked the logs and repaired the chinking where the moss had died and the thatch on the roof was repaired with straw from the wheat harvest. Papa told me this year I would go to the forest to cut trees with him. In Russia a shoemaker cannot make shoes in the winter. Leather shoes and boots are not worn in the winter, the temperature is too severe. All the people wear pressed fleece from sheep in the winter. We even wore these and they did keep our feet warm. It is the only footwear that will protect the foot and lower leg. Our family had to have an income during the winter, so we cut trees along with the other men in the village.

Just before winter set in, all the tools were cleaned, oiled and put away in their boxes during the winter. The tools were too precious to let anything happen to them. I was so excited. Papa had always gone to cut trees with other village men during the winter. This was the first time I had been allowed to go. The stories Papa told were so exciting, cutting trees and dragging them to the river and meeting men from other villages. Moses was going also. Papa said he would be needed. There was a sadness in Mama's eyes when we were preparing to leave. She looked at me and said, you are growing up, and you are not my little boy anymore. She then told me to take care of Moses. She had prepared food for us. Papa got his fishing gear, and Solomon helped me retrieve the boat from the loft in the barn. The boat was big enough for two people. I had never been in the boat in the water. The boat was kept turned upside down in the loft and many times I had climbed up and turned the boat over and pretended I was with Papa going down the river. My excitement was almost too much to bear.

The day arrived and, the first snow had already fallen. Four other men from Roshen were going with us. A neighbor had given Papa the use of two horses and our equipment was placed on them. Our equipment consisted of a tent, warm clothing and a special harness for dragging logs. The horses were a necessity. They carried the equipment that was used to drag the logs we cut. Mama gave me an extra long hug and told Moses and me to obey Papa. That was a strange request because I always obeyed Papa. Solomon would be at home to help Mama around the house. We began walking north from Roshen into the woods. We had exchanged our boots for fleece and they made a strange sound on the new snow as we walked. The woods enveloped us and blotted out part of the sun. I had often gone to these woods, but this trip was different. I was going over that hill I had always dreamed of. Papa talked more to Moses than to me. He kept pointing out landmarks to Moses. He said these would be very important because Moses would have to return to Roshen by himself.

Papa and me each carried a small axe in our belt. Moses wouldn't need one. This was for trimming branches off trees as they were felled and for felling highwaymen and fending off the occasional wolf pack that might wander by. Wolves didn't bother people too much. As long as there was plenty of small animals for them in the forest, they rarely came near the village. The area to which we were walking was about ten miles from Roshen, but in the winter, that was a long trip. The Black Forest was pine trees, and each year the men had to walk a little further from the village as more trees were cut. Not all trees were cut. They preferred trees that grew straight and tall with few branches. Each branch meant a knot. The trees with fewer branches had fewer knots. As we walked, I could see the stumps of trees that had been cut in previous years. The forest stretched on and on and a light snow began falling. A slight wind made the trees wave back and forth. It was magical. The trees, the snow and waving branches all seemed to beckon me to places unknown. My mind was reeling. I was with the men of the village to cut trees. I felt like a man.

Men from other villages joined us to cut trees. The snow was falling harder now and I knew this snow wouldn't melt. It would be on the ground until spring. The campsite was selected in an area where trees had been cut last year.

There was a total of 15 men to cut trees. Each village group would stay together. Papa and the men from Roshen began looking at trees. Three were selected. These were trees that were not good enough to be sold. They were crooked and gnarled. Each group felled three of these gnarled trees. They were about 50 feet long and the branches trimmed. Neither man nor beast can survive the Russian winter without some type of shelter. These three trees would be our shelter. We first built a snow bank. It had three sides and the open side faced south. The walls were about two feet thick and five feet tall. The three logs were then put inside the snow bank in the form of a square with one side open. The open side faced south away from the wind. The wind in winter was always from the north. The logs were placed on a bed of pine needles, which were then set on fire. The needles set the logs on fire, which would then burn down, and smolder. They would burn all night and form a pyramid of heat. We were very warm inside these three logs.

Each morning three more logs had to be cut to replace the ones burned the night before. The snow bank protected us from the winter wind. We spread our blankets on the

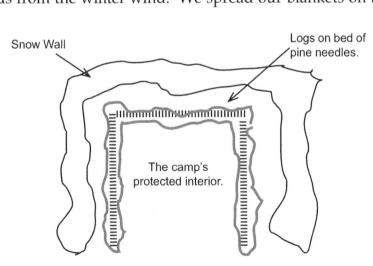

This is how three logs were arranged on the ground then set on fire with pine needles.

ground, unpacked and we were ready. Any meat was hung from a tree so the bears and wolves couldn't get it. The camp was ready. It had to always be ready in case of a sudden storm. Anyone caught out in one of those storms was dead. One would freeze to death in a matter of minutes in the wind. Papa told Moses and me to always be aware of which direction led to the camp. He talked very serious and explained this was a matter of life and death. He said if a sudden wind came up, it might whip up the snow and blind everyone. That was why we had to be aware of the location of the camp. I had to memorize the way to the camp. A path had been stomped into the snow, which would help, but a heavy blizzard would cover the path in a matter of minutes. Papa also told Moses he would spend most of his time in the camp to keep animals away and a fire going.

The camp had to be able to withstand any storm. If the wind increased, we would make the snow wall thicker so it would not collapse. One error in judgment on the Ukrainian winter could be fatal.

When the camp was ready, the men then began selecting areas where the trees would be cut. Each area was about 40 acres in size. All the trees in our 40 acres were ours to be cut and sold. This was also a safety factor. Within the area, there was no danger of a tree falling on anyone else. The trees had to be about 40 or 50 feet tall. Each man had his axe and saw sharpened, ready to cut and trim trees. The winter daylight was short and no time was wasted. Papa took the saw blade and the handles and I watched very carefully as he fitted the saw blade into the handles and tightened the bolts. The blade was about four feet long with a handle on each end. He looked at me and asked if I was ready to cut trees. I was so excited, I was being treated like a man. Of course I said yes. I could already hear the noise of men sawing trees in their areas. Papa told Moses to stay in camp. He explained this was a very important job. He would keep the camp ready if a storm suddenly approached. As we walked to our area, I watched two men on each end of the saw felling a tree.

I followed Papa and when he stopped, he said we were in our area. He said this was not going to be easy work. He further explained it was hard and my muscles would ache for a few days. He said I was used to making boots and shoes, not doing heavy work. He taught me the proper use of the saw. He instructed me where to place my hands on the handle and to draw the saw back. He said, never push the saw, I will pull it, then you pull it back. He selected a tree, and then instructed me on how to stay out of the way when the tree began to fall. He said that in a flash the tree could fall and I could be killed if I wasn't paying attention. Papa placed the blade against the tree and pulled and I pulled back. It took me several pulls, but I got the hang of it. It was going to be very tiring work. After about twenty minutes of pulling the blade back and forth, I heard a crack and Papa pulled the blade away from the tree. He took me by the shoulder and said, you have to watch which way the tree is going to fall, and always stay away. He yelled, "falling." This was a warning to anyone that might be in the area that a tree was falling and to be aware. Safety was his first concern. I watched in awe as the tree fell to earth. Papa then took his axe and began cutting off the branches. I followed suit and began hacking off branches. When Papa approached the top of the tree, he cut the top three or four feet off. The bottom of the tree was about three feet in diameter and the top of the tree was about six to eight inches in diameter.

Each man also marked the trees he cut. The mark resembled a branding iron. Papa's mark was the letter "A". After Papa cut a tree, he would place pine needles on the "A," then place it on the newly cut surface. With a hammer, he would hit the branding iron, which made a green "A" on the end of the log. Each man had a different mark.

With this method, each man was given credit for the trees he cut. After the cut tree was marked, it was dragged to a common collection point by the horses. The collection point was next to the River Dnieper that flowed not far from Roshen. Papa tried to cut trees close to the river. It could be very difficult to drag the logs. The first day ended and my arms and shoulders ached as we walked back to camp. Papa put his arm around me and said I had done a very good days work. Moses was waiting on us. The other men had set traps and rabbit was the main animal trapped. Either a wolf or a wild cat had eaten several of the rabbits. Some had brought meat just as we had, but they didn't have to obey the kosher laws, they could kill meat in the forest. Our supper consisted of a cold cabbage roll and hot tea. The sun was sinking and we bedded down in the tent. I was amazed how warm we were inside the perimeter of smoldering logs. It seemed I had just closed my eyes when Papa was shaking me and saying it is time to go to work. Oh, I was sore. He said the soreness would work out today or tomorrow. We ate and the first thing we did was cut a tree for the camp. The two other groups also cut a tree, so the camp was ready. We headed out and I saw Moses repairing the snow wall where the wind had eroded it. It was a slow start, but by noon, the soreness began to leave. We spent four days cutting, trimming, marking and dragging trees to the river.

At the river the logs were made into rafts. All logs with like markings were grouped. The bottom layer was made of ten logs lashed with ropes. The next layer had nine logs, the next eight and the top layer had five logs. Forty-five logs composed the raft. All the logs in our raft had the green "A" on the end. A spacer was in the middle of the raft, which created a space in the middle of the raft through all the layer of logs. Through this space was a long pole. This pole was made from a cull tree and was very important on the river. On top of the raft was all of our belongings and the boat. Our belongings consisted of a tent, clothing and food. All the other men caught and ate food in the forest, but we had to bring our food. Papa followed the dietary laws, so we could not kill meat in the forest. We only brought meat from animals the Rabbi had killed but we did catch fish in the river. I enjoyed fishing. I had been fishing with Papa on many occasions and I was good. We would dig in the ground and find grubs to use for bait. The other men in camp also fished with us because it was not easy to carry all your food, you had to live off the land while cutting trees.

Everyone helped construct the rafts and put the belongings on top. This would take a week or two of cutting and trimming the trees, dragging them and building the rafts. We erected the tent on top of the raft in which we slept while floating down the river. When each group had their raft ready, the flotilla began the journey. Papa and I each had a pole with which to propel the raft. Papa then told Moses this was the most important part of the journey for him. He would take the horses back home. Papa then asked Moses if he knew the way back home. It became clear why Papa was pointing out the landmarks along the way. Moses said he knew the way. Papa became very serious. He told Moses the horses would help him get home, but if he got lost, he would die in the forest. Moses' eyes grew very large at this thought but assured Papa he would make it home. We stood and watched Moses head back toward Roshen. In a few minutes another man headed out with his horses. Papa had already asked him to keep an eye on Moses. He said he would, but at a distance. He wanted Moses to be able to make the trip by himself.

Papa said the river was low and the water was not flowing fast. He said when the river was high, the journey was easy, but when low, it was work. We boarded the raft, and Papa pushed off with his pole. Papa was on the left side and I was on the right side of the raft. I don't know how deep the water was, but my pole was about twelve feet long. I would lift the pole out of the water and walk to the front of the raft and plunge it to the bottom of the river. Then I would push and walk to the back of the raft, lift the pole and walk to the front and the process would be repeated. I watched the forest slip by as we poled and watched the sunlight play on the ripples in the river. I never thought I would ever get this far from Roshen. As we poled down the river I watched the landscape pass and it was truly amazing how it changed. As we went down the river I watched the shadows the sun made on the logs of the raft and I thought of watching the sun rise over Roshen. I then thought of Moses. I could see him being attacked and mauled by wolves or a bear. I was sure I would never see him again. I did not know he was being watched over.

We passed other villages and it seemed everyone came out to greet us and send us on our way. As evening approached, we poled near a village and Papa took the small tree and pushed it into the space in the middle of the raft into the mud bottom of the river. Then he hammered the tree down and this anchored the raft for the night. The four rafts in the flotilla all anchored near the village and we went ashore. The villagers came to greet us. The men in our flotilla knew the people in the village from their previous trips and I was introduced to each man as the son of Abraham. Several other men had sons on their first trip and after the introductions, we were invited into their homes. Their homes looked just like our houses in Roshen. Food was provided for us and Papa explained we were Jews and this was no problem. The others in the group ate meat and we ate fish. We returned to the raft at sundown to ensure the safety of our trees. As the sun was coming up, Papa and I pulled the tree out of the mud and we began our trip again. This day we left the flotilla for one day. It was Friday and when we anchored for the night, we would spend the Sabbath in that spot. Papa did no work on the Sabbath. As we sat in the tent out of the sun, Papa told me stories of his childhood and my grandparents. He told of my grandfather, Simon who had been in the Russian army of Nicholas the First. We did not float that day, but we took off on Sunday and that evening we caught up with the flotilla. The other rafts did not float on Sunday.

We were floating to Poland. This is where the trees were sold. The trip took one week. The closer we came, more rafts appeared. We passed more and larger villages. I don't know the name of the city where we stopped. There were dozens of rafts waiting to be sold. The four rafts in our group stayed together. We spent the night there and the logs were sold the next day. Papa was paid and we took the boat and put our belongings in it for the trip back to Roshen. Our trees would be sold all over Europe to be made into furniture, clocks, houses and anything else made of wood. As soon as we were loaded, the four small boats began the trip back up river. Instead of poles, we had oars. Our group stayed together for safety if for no other reason. The round trip took two weeks. It was the most exciting time of my life. We returned to our home and I was glad to see Moses and know he made it home safe. We spent two days at home and off we went to the forest to cut more trees and float to Poland. During the winter, Papa would cut enough trees to make four or five rafts. It depended on how much money Papa needed. We really didn't need much money in Roshen, the village used the barter system. But Papa was always working, even if he didn't need money, he was cutting trees. There were times, he would help a villager who had no one to help him cut trees. If Papa needed help, there was always a villager to help. Between making shoes and boots and cutting trees in the winter, life was good in Roshen.

Most of the other families in Roshen raised wheat. As I said before, the Ukraine was the breadbasket of Russia. The wheat raised was Russian Red, but Uncle Herman said it was called Turkey Red in the United States. All farming was done by hand. The soil was plowed using a walking plow, the seed broadcast and harvested by hand. We didn't raise wheat, but Papa was always in the fields helping others. He never asked for payment for his labor. He always said there were more important things than money. For his work, Papa was well respected in the village.

Wheat harvest was always exciting. The whole village took part in this. The women cooked for the men as they worked the fields. Of course Mama cooked for Papa. The whole village knew this and respected Papa for his beliefs. The wheat was cut by hand with a scythe, bound and then shocked. Harvest began in July and took several weeks. There were about 200 acres of wheat grown around the village. After the wheat was shocked, it went through a "sweat" and then was time to be thrashed. In the middle of the village, the bundles were laid in a row with all the heads pointed inward. The middle of the street was turned yellow by the wheat. The line of wheat was almost 200 feet long. The men had flails, a pole about six feet long with a leather thong attached to the end. The thong was about one

This is how the wheat was thrashed. It was all done by hand.

foot long. On the end of this thong was attached a piece of wood also one foot long. The men would walk around and around the wheat, flailing the wheat, thrashing the grain. It took about one hour to thrash the pile.

The straw was removed and new bundles were placed on the ground to be flailed. The straw was kept in bundles to repair the roofs on the houses. Each time two or three piles had been thrashed, the women came in with baskets and gathered the grain. Then the thrashing continued. I was 12 years old when I began thrashing with the men. The wheat was then distributed to the villagers. Each family received their fair share. This was also a busy time for Papa in making and repairing the boots for the men in the harvest. Wheat Harvest was hard on the boots.

Before winter set in, each chimney was cleaned and checked. A branch was used to clean the chimney. A rope was tied to the branch, which was about the size of the chimney. It was lowered down into the chimney. At the bottom, another rope was tied to the branch. The branch was then pulled up and down through the chimney, cleaning out the soot. This made sure the soot would not catch on fire and burn the house. Where the chimney went through the roof straw, wood was placed over the straw. This also helped prevent fire. The straw was very flammable and I remember several houses burning and the families burning to death. The roof had caught on fire and before the families could escape, the roof came crashing down, then there was no escape. This was the time Papa prepared the winter bed. This bed was built between the oven and the wall. The entire family slept in this winter bed. It was easier to keep warm in this winter bed. When the fire in the oven burned down, Solomon, Moses and I would sleep on top of the oven. This was the warmest place in the house.

The chickens were brought inside the house during the winter and while we slept on top of the stove, the chickens roosted under it. The stove was built about six inches off the floor, just enough space for the chickens. When our cow was about to calf, we would also bring her in the house. If we didn't bring her in, she would try to hide her calf and several times the calf became fodder for wolves. It was the nature of the cow to hide the calf but not during the Russian Winter.

We were warm in that house during the winter. I think back on those winter days, the whole family sleeping in one bed, with chickens and a cow in the house. There was lots of love in the house, but it was not displayed. Papa was very stoic and did not show emotion, but it was good to be a Russian Jew, alive at that time. I would watch the geese flying over and that sparked my imagination. Where were they flying? I wanted to join them on their journeys. Papa spoke of Rovno, the mayor spoke of Minsk and I had heard of Odessa. The world was waiting.

Chapter Two

The Heartbreak of Leaving Roshen

I remember the day of the bear. It was in the early spring and Papa had two beehives in the forest and it was Solomon's and my job to check the hives. Every family had bees, but they had to be kept in the forest. Bears were attracted by the honey and it was too dangerous to keep them near the village. Our hives were about one mile into the woods. They were on a wooden platform about 15 high in a tree. Holes were drilled in the platform then spikes were hammered into the holes. The spikes pointed down and when a bear tried to climb the tree, the spikes would hit him in the head and nose and he couldn't get to the hives. He had to use both paws to climb the tree and it keeps him from using one paw to rake the hive off the platform. But one bear had been getting hives. Three hives had been destroyed. Claw marks on the tree identified the culprit as a bear. Sugar was very costly and the honey was used as a substitute.

Solomon and I approached the tree and there were claw marks on the tree, and one hive was gone. It was on the ground and had been torn apart. We ran and told Papa. This made four hives gone. Papa said the bear had to be destroyed. He would eventually destroy all the hives and the bees would be destroyed or leave, depending if the queen survived. Six villagers gathered to kill the bear. Papa said I could go with him and watch. We were forbidden to help kill the bear, unless another human life was in danger. Each man had a pole about eight feet long with a knife blade attached to the end. The blade had been sharpened on both sides. Papa carried a pole just case he was needed. He ordered me to stay out of the way and not to attract the attention of the bear. Mama did not like the idea of me going at all. She told Papa it was too dangerous. I had never heard Mama talk to Papa like this and he never answered her. She looked from him to me and turned away. Papa was putting on a coat when he murmured that I was growing up. I put on my coat also and as I walked out the door behind Papa, I looked back and saw the look of fear on Mama's face. That look sent shivers down my back. I had never seen a look like that, not even when I went to cut trees with Papa.

Mr. Kereowski had been volunteered to kill the bear. He had killed several bears in the past and was the best qualified. The Russian bear was not an animal to be lightly reckoned with. It is ferocious and can be deadly. A wounded bear is one of the most vicious animals on earth. Mr. Kereowski had his dog with him and I was wide eyed with anticipation. The group approached our bee tree and I was walking behind Papa with Alexis. He told me he had seen a bear killed once. He said that at the end he felt sorry for the bear. I couldn't understand this. The bear was destroying the village supply of honey. The men stood around the destroyed hive and the dog was sniffing and becoming excited. He was getting the scent of the bear. Papa turned to me with a deadly serious look on his face and told me to stay out of the way and if things went bad to run back to village and not to look back. I had never run from danger and I didn't like the idea of running now. Besides, what could go wrong?

The dog had the scent, and was released from his leash and he took off through the woods. It was difficult to keep up with the dog. We all were running at break neck speed. I don't think I had run this fast this long in my life. Papa had me running in front of him. When we started he told Alexis and me both to stay in front of him because if we didn't stay with the group we would be a good meal for a pack of wolves.

My legs ached and it seemed we had been running for hours, but it was only 35 or 40 minutes. I was in good shape and kept up good for my nine years. The dog "sounded off." The bear was "treed" in a cave. Papa got in front of us and told us to stay behind now and explained this was the most dangerous part. The dog kept barking at the cave entrance, which was about four feet across. The soft earth still showed the bear prints going into the cave. It was a large bear. How to get the bear out of the cave and if it was a female, did she have cubs?

The cave was situated on the north side of a small hill, about 30 feet high. We walked along the face of the hill and even climbed to see if there was another entrance to the cave. We didn't find one. A small pine tree was cut and we gathered dead branches. These were pushed into the mouth of the cave, the dead branches on bottom and the newly cut tree on top. The pile was set of fire. The leaves and dead branches burned fast and the pine tree began smoking. We would smoke the bear out.

The dog continued barking while the fire grew. Smoke began belching out of the cave and we kept looking for smoke to come out from another entrance we hadn't discovered. Papa told us that when the bear comes out he was going to be mad and for us to stay out of the way. He said he didn't have time to watch the bear and watch us. Alexis and I moved back from the cave entrance and stood next to a tree. I realized the bear could climb the tree, but I didn't know what else to do. I was expecting when the bear did come out he would attack and kill Papa and then the rest of the men. For the first time I felt an impending doom and it was an unfamiliar emotion. In a few minutes the group realized there was not another entrance to the cave and water was thrown on the fire to produce more smoke. The men moved back and Mr. Kereowski took hold of the dog. He knew if the bear attacked the dog, it would be no contest. The dog would be killed instantly.

A large tree was about 20 feet from the entrance of the cave and he took up a position near the tree with his dog. Papa was behind the tree, ready to take the dog. Suddenly it seemed the mouth of the cave exploded. A huge, bellowing hulk came crashing out through the smoke and fire. It raised on its hind legs and I thought it was going to reach to the sky. Alexis and I both shrank back behind the tree. The dog was pulling at its collar, ready to attack the bear. The bear bellowed in the direction of the dog and made a movement towards them. Mr. Kereowski motioned and Papa reached from behind the tree and took the dog by the leash. He then retreated within a safe distance. A muzzle was placed on the dog to keep him quiet.

The bear thundered down on all fours and lumbered toward Mr. Kereowski and I knew he would be torn limb from limb by the bear. He animal stood almost ten feet tall. I had seen bears in the forest before, but they had never been threatening. He waited until the bear was just four or five feet from him then he darted behind the tree, his sharpened pole at the ready. To attack, the bear has to rear up on his hind legs. He did so and Mr. Kereowski moved further behind the tree. Two men had approached the bear from behind, but out of sight, just in case help was needed. Mr. Kereowski had walked backwards almost completely behind the tree, always keeping the bear in view. He stopped and stepped away from the tree.

The bear had gone back on all fours and then reared up to attach. At this moment, the spear was plunged into the bear's stomach and Mr. Kereowski cut upwards. Blood gushed from the wound and the bear roared in agony and rage. He went down on all fours again and Mr. Kereowski began backing up again around the tree. The bear kept roaring in agony and began pulling hair from its body and stuffing into the wound. It seems the animals of the forest joined in with the roar of the bear. I had never heard such noises from the animals and birds. It seemed they knew death was imminent. I knew a wounded bear was dangerous and I was fearing for everyone's safety, yet I felt pity for him. His bellows roared in my ears until I covered them to block the noise. It was the most hideous noise I had heard in my life.

The bear charged, reared up and the pole was plunged into his abdomen again. Another bellow of pain. The noise became insufferable and I wanted to divert my eyes, but I couldn't. I was mesmerized by Mr. Kereowski and the bear. I watched the spear plunge into the body five or six times. The last time, the bear was disemboweled. It fell to the ground, the bellows and roars were now whimpers of agony and I was at the point of tears. I still couldn't look away. Papa and the other men approached the bear. It was just a hulk lying on the ground. I could see it raise and lower as it inhaled and exhaled. No noise came from it now. I had watched the Rabbi kill animals, but it was quick and merciful and I had seen nothing such as this. It was a slow and torturous end of a life. I saw Mr. Kereowski raise his pole and plunge it into the heart of the bear. One last bellow was emitted and then silence.

The hulk laid there and the forest was silent. It seems all the creatures became silent for the life that was just blotted out. I looked at Alexis and tears filled his eyes. I felt a tear run down my cheek. The bear had to be killed, yet I felt pity and remorse. I had been taught to respect all forms of life and to watch such a magnificent creature die in such agony was more than I could bear. I walked up and stood next to Papa. He never showed emotion, but he put his arm around my shoulder. He knew what I was feeling, then he said, "it is over."

The bear was butchered and the meat was divided among the men. Our dietary laws forbade us to eat the meat. It would have to be killed by the Rabbi in order to be Kosher. The fat was taken back to be rendered into lard for cooking. Even if the meat was clean, I couldn't have eaten any. I knew the suffering and agony of the bear would be relived by me each time I saw the meat.

On the way back to the village, the death of the bear haunted me. I usually was very talkative with Papa, but I walked in silence. I thought perhaps I could set out an extra hive for the bears, but how to teach a bear to take only honey from that hive. The bear was one of God's creatures and I watched it die. My sleep was haunted for weeks. I loved honey on Mama's bread, but I couldn't eat the honey. Every time I tried, I heard the death throes of the bear. Papa explained several times the bear had to be destroyed and I knew this. I just wished I hadn't gone. Mama talked to me also. She said it was part of life in Roshen and it would happen again as it had in the past. She then told me stories of her father-in-law, Grandpa Kerbel in the army of Nicholas the First fighting in Hungary. She said he used to tell stories when she and Papa were first married. He had killed many men in the wars in Hungary and was haunted for years by those deaths. She asked what would be more difficult, to kill another man or a bear stealing honey. I wanted to tell her I think I could kill a man easier than a bear. The bear was an animal, the men would be trying to kill me. I didn't say anything, I knew she was trying to make the situation better. No matter what they said, I still felt sorry for the bear, but realized it had to die.

Papa said I was a dreamer. He told me he had heard enough of my feelings for the bear and did not want to hear anymore. Perhaps I was a dreamer. I always wondered what was over the next hill, where the logs went from Poland and where the geese were flying. Solomon and Moses were more sedate than me. They weren't dreamers. They were better qualified to take over our ten acre farm. Roshen was a good place to grow up, but I wanted to see what was over the horizon. I knew Mama and Papa both worried about the farm. I was expected to take it, being the oldest.

Jews could not own land in Russia, it was a way and fact

of life. We owned ten acres at Roshen. Grandpa Kerbel had served in the army of Nicholas the First and fought many battles for the Czar and Mother Russia. For his service, he was given forty acres in Roshen. He had four sons and each received ten acres. The other three sons moved on to Minsk, Moscow and Kiev and gave up their land and had families of their own. Papa was the only one to stay in Roshen and we lost contact with Papa's brothers but he said they moved to the city and opened large shoe shops. He said he preferred the life in Roshen to the large cities. I never realized the Jews that came to our house during the Rabbi's visit did not own their land. We were a rare breed in Russia, Jews that owned land.

The Black Forest of the Ukraine was an excellent area to hunt bear. Men had come for centuries for the sport. Once or twice a year a hunting party from Moscow would come through. Those were exciting days to see strangers from Moscow. I heard they were some type of nobility, related to the Czar. I was always excited when they came, but they paid no attention to a little Jewish boy in the local village. I think it was late August of 1897 when a group of soldiers came to town. There was an air of excitement in the village. Soldiers didn't come to Roshen often. Something was up. A captain led the group. He met with the mayor and they talked for several hours. As soon as the soldiers left, the mayor called a meeting. The Czar was coming to Roshen to hunt bear. I first thought of Mr. Kereowski and the bear and I shivered. But this was the Czar. I had heard of him and sat in his chair in the church, and we had his photograph in our house, but he was really coming to my village. The Czar looked very handsome in his uniform and the Czarina was stunning in her gown. I looked at that photograph many times. Alexandra was not coming, but her brother was. He would be with the Czar. The mayor was excited. He was planning a large reception and have the Czar speak to the town. He even wanted his brother-in-law to speak.

He was the Grand Duke Ernst Ludwig von Hessen from Darmstadt, Germany, in the state of Hesse. Until then I never realized the Czarina was not Russian, she was German. I would get to see the Czar and a German prince. I was doubly excited. The Czar would arrive in two weeks. The town was cleaned, every house was put in order for the royal visit. Food was prepared and all was in readiness.

Then the soldiers returned the day before the Czar arrived. I thought my world would come crashing down. The mayor was told to keep everyone in their homes while the hunting party passed through town. It seemed there had been rumors of an attempt on the life of the Czar and this was for his protection. Protection from Roshen? We were a farming village, we were no threat to the Czar. The mayor was visibly upset. He had made lavish plans to meet the Czar and these had been dashed. The food was given

Photograph Czar Nicholas II taken in 1897.

back to the families and a feeling of disappointment that bordered on rage filled the streets of Roshen. Evening came and more soldiers arrived in town. Oh, I wanted to see the Czar. I knew now I was a dreamer. I thought of my trip with Papa on the log raft and my walks in the forest. This was the extent of my travels. The Mayor had been to Minsk and the Czar had traveled all over Europe. What did the Czar have to fear from a small boy in a Ukrainian village?

All the windows in all the houses were shuttered and soldiers lined the street. I turned my head sideways to look at the soldiers through the cracks in the shudders. There was a soldier about every 20 feet. They stood like statues with their rifles. Some had horses and some were on foot. Mama told me to get away from the window. I would walk a few steps away, then when she wasn't looking, quickly return to try to look again. She finally gave up knowing I was not leaving the window. I was angry at the soldiers. This was a once in a lifetime chance and the soldiers told me to stay in my house. I knew every other house had people peeking through the shutters. If I were caught, what would happen? Would I be flogged or shot? But I was willing to take that chance, I wanted to see the Czar.

I heard something outside. The soldiers had been standing for about three hours when an order was barked. All the soldiers snapped to attention. In a few minutes I heard the rumble of wagon wheels. I was craning and trying to force the shutter open just a bit more to get a better view. I saw an open wagon with people and behind it was an enclosed wagon followed by another open wagon. I assumed the Czar and the prince were in the enclosed wagon. The wagons passed very quickly and they were gone. As they passed, the soldiers with horses mounted and rode off. A wagon picked up the foot soldiers and they took off in pursuit of the Czar. The Czar was in Roshen for no more than a few minutes. Just a few minutes of fame. I felt cheated, all I saw was an enclosed wagon. I turned and caught Mama trying to peek through a shutter. She gave me a sheepish look, she had been caught doing what she didn't want me to do.

For the next two weeks there was a patrol of soldiers either in the village or on the outskirts. We were forbidden to go to the forest. I wanted so bad to run into the forest and meet the Czar, to shake his hand, and to go back to Moscow with him for a visit. The cattle and sheep could not be taken out while the hunting party was in the area. We were told to stay in our homes and shutter our windows and just as quickly as the Czar came, he left. The village returned to normal, but how can Roshen return to normal when the Czar had been there?

The Czar was a great man, he had to be. He ruled all of Russia. In Roshen, the mayor had a big job and the government in Minsk was larger. I had no comprehension of how large Russia was and how important the job of Czar was. Suddenly in two days, a group of soldiers returned to Roshen. I knew the Czar was returning when the mayor called another meeting. Papa went to the meeting and I stayed at home with the family. The meeting began at 2:00 in the afternoon and lasted one hour. Papa came home and I knew something was wrong. I had never seen him look as bad. He left the house as he always did, brave and bold, but he returned he looked like an old broken man. I couldn't understand. Without saying a word he took Mama outside. We kids remained inside and I wanted to go out to see what was going on. For Papa to look so bad something horrible had happened. Perhaps there had been an accident. Was the Czar injured or even dead? I had to know what was going on, but I didn't dare go outside. To go outside would be disobedience and that was unheard of. Moses and I were putting pitch on the boat because Papa and I would be returning to the forest to cut more trees in a few days. The door opened and Mama was crying. I knew the Czar was dead.

Mama went and sat at the table and placed her head in her hands. I could see her tremble as she was crying. Papa called us together. I was ready for the worst. Papa had always been a kind and happy man, but none of this showed now. He said, "We have to leave Roshen." I didn't understand. Why did we have to leave Roshen? He continued that the mayor said the German prince had such a good time on the bear hunt and told this to the Czar. The prince then said he wished he had a place like this in Germany to hunt bear. The Czar had just given this area to the German Royal family. This area was no longer Russia. I still didn't understand. How could the Czar give our land away? This had been our land for three generations. Papa said the entire village had one year to move. We have to

This is a photograph of the Grand Duke Ernst Ludwig to whom the Czar gave our land. This photo was taken in 1905 by Jacob Hilsdorf.

be gone by the end of wheat harvest next year. Twelve other villages in the area had to leave also. This was now a private hunting reserve for the brother-in-law of the Czar. Suddenly I didn't want to see the Czar. I understood and wished I didn't. I had always wanted to travel, but keep roots in Roshen. My roots had just been pulled up. The world didn't appear so appetizing as it did two minutes ago. How the world can change in the wink of an eye.

In December I would be nine years old. Roshen had been my entire world and it was a good solid place. Mama and Papa were both strong, but the news had hurt them and it hurt me to see them. Losing the land was the worst part. What would become of us, the shoe shop, the family? The next few weeks drug by. There seemed to be a veil over the village. Our sentiments were shared with the entire population. Disbelief reigned. In another meeting it was told that the villagers would be given land elsewhere. Everyone except the Jews, because Jews couldn't own land. Papa was devastated again. At first there was hope we would get land elsewhere, but that was dashed.

All the Gentiles would be given land outside the area set aside for the German prince. Their land would be replaced but since Jews could not own land, they had none to replace. But we were different, we owned land. The Czar had given land to Grandpa Kerbel, didn't they understand this? I asked Papa. He said he had already told them about his father's military service. It didn't matter, Jews could not own land. I wanted to ask again and Papa shouted at me, something he never did. He told me to keep quiet, we had lost the land and had no where to go. He said we might as well become Gypsies. The photograph of the Czar disappeared from the house.

Papa continued making shoes. He said we had one more year to live here, then we had to find a place. Papa always knew what to do, but this time he was lost. Papa was the cornerstone of the family and Mama was the strength of the family and both seemed to be lost. I heard Mama crying in bed at night. Her cries were joined by those of Guerta and Rosa. Even the men in the village were shocked that we would not be given land elsewhere. Papa said Russia was a big place, what is ten acres to the Czar. He was becoming a bitter man. He was raising his voice more often and I saw him slam his fist against the barn one morning. I had never seen him do this. We were also leaving the cemetery. Our dead would be left behind. No more would I be able to visit the graves of my grandparents. Suddenly there seemed to be a daily stream of people visiting the graves of family members and a constant wail was heard from the graves. The cemetery became the place where people vented their anger.

Rabbi Kautzman came for a visit and it wasn't the Sabbath. This had to be more bad news. I had gone from admiring the Czar to almost despising him. He was tearing our family apart. After one or two weeks, Mama seemed to gather her strength and she said we would survive this. As I said she was the strength of the family and this made Papa settle down. I had never seen him so unsettled. He and the Rabbi were out by the barn talking. I saw Papa slam his fist against the barn again. The Rabbi was a great man. He could talk to anyone. He could calm a raging storm and make a vicious man feel like a child. As for me, for a nine year old, I thought he could walk with God.

They came to the house and Papa said we were moving to Odessa. The Rabbi said there was a large Jewish population there and most of the Jews in the other villages would be moving to Odessa. He continued that with the influx of population, another shoe shop may be needed. A lecture followed. He reminded Papa that the Czar owned Russia and it was his to do with as he wished. We may not like it, but the Jews and Gentiles both were powerless to do anything. Then he said God would provide for us. The last thing he said was that we could move peacefully or be forced out by the military. The townspeople knew us and respected us but soldiers from Moscow probably would not hesitate to kill a Jew family that was disputing the order of the Czar.

After the Rabbi left, Papa said everything is true. We have to leave peacefully and go to Odessa. Mama said we will survive. We were healthy and Papa was a good shoemaker and had two sons who were good shoemakers and we would have a good life in Odessa. She then told us to look into our hearts and think of our life in Roshen and never, never forget what we have here. The village had been her source of strength and she would take that strength with her. As long as she was alive Roshen would be alive. I decided then that I would keep Roshen alive inside of me also.

My whole outlook changed. Every time I went to the forest, I observed everything. I listened to the birds and watched the animals. I went to the river and watched and listened to the water cascade over the rocks. I then watched the clouds in the sky, thinking perhaps God would give me a reason why this was happening. I began talking to nature, trees, rocks, animals even the grass. I went to the cave where the bear had been killed. I sat down by the tree where he died and I cried and cried and screamed to God, "Why?" I could not find a reason and no answer came.

The year came and went. Mama tied to keep our life as normal as possible. Papa made shoes and I tried, but my heart was not in it. Papa corrected several shoes I made, but he never mentioned my mistakes. It seemed the heart had been torn out of the village and it was dying. Roshen was dying and in a few weeks it would be dead. Our business increased the last month. It seemed every villager wanted a new pair of shoes. Many said they would miss the Kerbel shoe. I realized the end was near and was determined to leave Roshen proud. I began making a good shoe like I used to. Papa mentioned this and he was proud of me.

Mama, Guerta and Rosa had been packing items for almost two weeks. We couldn't take everything, just what would fit in our wagon. I had a lifetime of memories to take and a few possessions. Wheat harvest was approaching. This was the last act for the village. As in generations past, the women cooked for the workers. I went with Papa to the fields with a scythe. This would be my first and only wheat harvest. In previous years I was busy making shoes. Papa instructed me on how to hold the wheat stalks then pull the scythe across to cut and stack them. It seemed ironic for him to be instructing me on the last wheat harvest ever to be held in the village.

After working for about one hour, my back began to ache. I wasn't used to this type of work. I rose up and saw villagers throughout the fields cutting wheat. Wheat had been grown in this field for generations. No one knew when there was not a village of Roshen, it had existed for centuries. The women joined the men after the food was cooked and began cutting wheat. As one group cut, another group gathered the wheat to make the bundles and yet another group shocked the wheat. All during that first day, I saw small groups of women clustered talking. I was near one group and they were talking about this was the last harvest and the village would be torn apart and everyone would be going in different directions. These families had lived and died in this village. That evening there was another pilgrimage to the cemetery. Papa went to visit Grandma and Grandpa. What would happen to these graves? Would we ever be allowed to return or would this be Germany forever.

The harvest lasted two weeks and then the thrashing began. The first cut wheat had gone through the sweat and was dry enough. Wagons were brought to the fields and the shocks placed carefully aboard. I had never heard such a silence during thrashing season. In the past it was as a holiday. The whole village participated, but this was different. This act of thrashing was the absolute last the village would ever do. The shocks were laid in the street as they had in the past the flailing began. The thrashing lasted two weeks, just as the harvest had. The wheat straw was even placed next to the houses as if the roofs were to be repaired. They would never be used, not by us anyway. The mayor called a meeting on the last day of thrashing. The entire village came. The grain was to be divided among the families. It was just like a funeral. In fact it was the funeral of the village. Each family took their share of the grain and silently returned to their homes to pack the last items and leave forever.

The sun rose on a beautiful July day. The last day of Roshen and soldiers entered the village. The mayor met them and assured them that every family had packed and was prepared to leave. The soldiers tried to be friendly, and the commander of the group apologized again and again to the mayor. He said if he had his way, this would never have happened. He did not agree with giving Russian soil to Germany. The soldiers left and the first families began leaving. There were farewells, hugs and tears, but everyone seemed reserved as if on the brink of an impending disaster.

Hunting season was approaching and we had to be gone in a matter of days. Papa said he wanted to get the wagon loaded and get out. There was no use dragging the whole affair out. In two days, he hitched the two horses to the wagon and began putting carefully packed bundles in the wagon. Mama had a bundle she would carry. In that bundle was the oil lamp. There were other lamps in the village now, but it was still her prized possession. This bundle would never leave her sight. Moses, Solomon and I helped load the wagon Papa said that was all the horses could pull. We were leaving all the furniture Papa had made, the beds, most of the bedding and a lifetime of memories. Papa said the time had come. He took his jacket and hat and walked out the door and climbed onto the wagon.

All of us kids walked out and Mama stood in the middle of the room and began crying. Papa bellowed at her to get out, it was time. She walked out and reverently closed the door and I helped her onto the wagon next to Papa. All our animals were given to the villagers. We wouldn't need them in Odessa. I had one year to prepare for this moment, but I was not ready. Papa took the reins and gave them a flip and the journey began. Mama lowered her head and began to cry softly. Papa told her not to cry. He looked straight ahead. Mama looked back and I turned my head to look. Papa never flinched. He stared straight ahead. She asked him if he was not going to look back. He said he had his last look locked in his heart forever. We moved down the street. The few villagers left came out and bid us farewell. All the women were crying and all the men were very stoic. There were soldiers in the village and I tried to pretend they were guarding us as they had the Czar that day. The day the Czar came through Roshen seemed a whole lifetime away. I took one last look as the road turned and the house vanished from my view. I saw Alexis and his family. He said we would meet again and I agreed. I did not see him for many years. They were moving to Kiev and we were going to Odessa.

Odessa, that seemed a whole world away. It was about 500 miles away, but it could have been 5,000 or 50,000 miles. The journey was a sad one. Papa said the German Royal Family would be living in our homes to hunt bear. The rest of the year the village would probably be empty except for the wolves and bears. He shook his head and became silent. The trip to Stolbtsy took three days. I walked most of the way next to the wagon. As I walked I watched the wheel turn and knew we were getting further and further away from Roshen. As I walked I wondered what Mama and Papa were thinking. Our whole life had been turned upside down. We all slept under the wagon and Papa was always on guard. Each night I could hear Mama crying softly as Papa held her and this tore at my heart. I still couldn't understand why this was happening. Mama was the kindest person I ever knew and I had never heard her cry like this. She never hurt anyone and to hear her cry tore at me. Every tear she shed hardened my heart more. No one felt like eating much during those three days. In the daytime Mama put up a good front for us. We knew it was a front and she realized we knew. It seemed better if we all pretended. As we traveled I watched the landscape and thought of the landscape on the river when Papa and I were on the raft, but this was different. The raft was a happy time, but this was a terrible time.

This part of the Ukraine was rural and the houses were few and far between but the closer we came to Stolbsty, the more numerous the houses became. Stolbtsy was a big city. It had a population of 20,000 people and even had streets paved with cobblestones. I had never seen such a sight. Paved streets and oil lamps were at regular intervals along the street. I listened as the wheels of our cart made a clicking sound on the cobblestones. I had momentarily forgotten Roshen. We drove straight to the train station and Papa purchased the tickets. I had never seen train tracks more less a real train and now I was going to ride on one. My excitement could not be contained. Mama and Papa joined in my joy and I think it helped relieved the pain they were suffering.

I was looking at the train station and amazed how large it was. I had never seen a building made of such fine stones. They were smooth and polished and fit together so well and the ceiling was at least 15 feet over my head. There was one small barn in Roshen made of stacked stone but they were not as fine or as large as the stones in the station. I was admiring the station when the train pulled in. I was amazed again how large it was and how much noise it made. The engine was belching smoke and creaked and groaned to a stop. We were inside the station when the train stopped and I was startled by steam pouring out from around the wheels. It made a whistling sound and I stood watching this steam pour out.

People began getting off the train and when they cleared the platform, the doors were opened and we approached the train. I saw men putting our baggage on the train with the baggage of other passengers. Our horses were put in another car with the cart but one table had to be left at the station because there was no room. Papa said the horses were much more important than the table because he could always make another table. We took our seats and Papa took Moses to the car with the horses to quiet the horses. I know the horses were as nervous as I was because they had never seen a train either.

The train whistle blew and I saw a conductor look along the train, signal the engineer and he jumped on. The car we were in jumped a little then began moving. I could hear the engine puffing faster and faster and the car began moving faster in unison with the engine. I had never seen such a method of transportation. The train was moving very fast, the fastest I had ever traveled and it began to slow down. I asked Papa if we were already at Odessa. He told me, no and we pulled to a stop next to a tower. I was looking out the window and watched a man pull a piece of pipe and Papa told me the engine had to take on water. Papa took me to the car with the horses and Moses and I exchanged places. Every time the train stopped to take on water, Solomon, Moses and I traded places. We took turns riding with the horses to calm them.

I asked Papa how fast the train could travel and he told me about twenty miles per hour. I didn't think a speed that fast was possible. It took as long to travel from Stolbsty to Odessa as it did from Roshen to Stolbsty, three days. It was a good trip and took my mind off why we were moving. The countryside and trees zipped by and everyone in the fields waved at the train and I waved back. The wheels made rhythmic noises on the tracks and made it easy to sleep. Mama and Papa didn't sleep much though.

As we approached Odessa, the houses became more numerous just as they did outside Stolbsty. The single track became a double track and then we passed a train going in the opposite direction and it just flew by. The double track became a triple track then I saw poles with wires strung between them. Papa told me they were electric wire and many of the trees we had cut in the forest were now used to make the poles which held the wires and I felt pride that I helped make the poles. The houses were now next to each other, block after block. Streets crossed the tracks and there were wagons and buggies waiting for the train to pass at every crossing. I had never seen so many wagons and fancy buggies. I think I was going to like Odessa.

I then saw a wagon with no horses. It had a line attached to the wire overhead and was riding on the tracks like a train. Papa said it must be one of the electric cars he had heard about. I had heard of electricity but never seen what it could do. There were so many houses, streets, and people in Odessa. The train began slowing and we pulled into the station. The station at Odessa was so much larger than the station in Stolbsty. This station was also made of the smooth stones and there were carvings on the wall and the a life-size portrait of the Czar and Carina. As I looked at the portraits, I felt anguish of why we were making this journey.

I was admiring the station and watching the people. I had never seen so many people in one spot. The whole town of Roshen could fit inside this train station. Papa saw a man carrying a sign with "Kerbel" on it. Papa identified himself to the man carrying the sign. The man's name was Denetsdki and he was to take us to the Synagogue to meet the Rabbi. We were going to a real Synagogue. I had never seen a Synagogue. Our belongings were taken off the train and another man was with Mr. Denetsdki with a wagon to pick up our belongings. Papa told us boys to stay with the horses as he helped Mama, Gueti and Rosa into the wagon. Just like me, the horses had never been in such a large city and Papa told us to keep the blinders on the horses. I don't know who was the most nervous, the horses or me.

Papa returned with the Rabbi. His name was Blatt and was a very nice man. He had several other families from the Synagogue to greet us. Then I saw Rabbi Kautzman. I was so happy to see him, someone that I knew. There were several boys my age and we were introduced and they were going to make life easier in Odessa. Rabbi Blatt took Solomon, Moses and me to the school at the Synagogue. There was also a boarding school where boys that lived outside of Odessa could stay. Mr. and Mrs. Popolinski met mama, Gueti and Rosa at the Synagogue and we were informed we would be living with them until we found a place of our own. Papa had a job waiting for him at a shoe shop owned by Mr. Shipirski, five blocks from the waterfront and port at Odessa.

Chapter Three
The Shoe Shop in Odessa

I stood outside the gate and marveled at the sight. I was looking at a real Synagogue. The fence around the Synagogue was made of iron and about eight feet tall. The fence surrounded the Synagogue and school, which covered about four acres. This was the Brodsky Synagogue and Papa told me there were two other Synagogues in Odessa. The building was made of cut stone just as the train station but this was much older. The windows were dark from the candle smoke and dark streaks ran down the stones from the top of the walls. The roof was black slate and centuries of rainfall and snow had streaked the walls. The gate was open and we walked in. All three of us boys were there to be enrolled in the school. Rabbi Blatt had a kind face and took us to the school and I was still in awe. The Rabbi took us through the front door of the Synagogue and the ceiling had to be 30 feet overhead. We turned right inside the door and went to the school. I wanted to stay in the Synagogue because I had never seen such a building.

Mr. Yeniscavich was a teacher in the school. He greeted us, the Rabbi left and we walked down a hall. Mr. Yeniscavich told us there were about 80 boys in the school and we passed several rooms where boys were studying. I had two years of schooling in Roshen but it was in a Christian School. Solomon and Moses had never attended a school. We were far behind the other boys in studies but we were advanced in other areas. The first week we had studies from the Torah but we had trouble paying attention because we were the new boys in school. Toward the end of that first week, we were to have a "Show and Tell." I couldn't think of a topic and Mr. Yeniscavich stopped me after class and asked if I could show how to make a pair of shoes. I was ecstatic. I told him I would bring my tools and ask Papa for a piece of leather to make a shoe. When I got home, Papa had a piece of leather laid out for me. How did Papa know I was going to ask for a piece of leather? I didn't ask him.

I arrived the next day with my tools and leather and the boys in the class seemed confused. Mr. Yeniscavich told the boys that I was a shoemaker and he had asked if could demonstrate how to make a shoe. I realized then that "Show and Tell" was not part of the normal class. Mr. Yeniscavich asked Rudolph to come to the front of the class and asked if I would make the shoes to fit Rudolph. A chair was put on the table in front of the class and Rudolph sat in the chair. His shoes were very worn and I took them off. The boys gathered around and Mr. Yeniscavich asked me to explain everything I was doing. I first measured his feet and told the class that the shoe had to be made for each foot because your two feet are different. I explained how I measured each foot and wrote down the dimensions. I then took the leather and explained how to cut the leather to make the shoe. Rudolph and I were in front of the class for almost two hours. The session was over and the shoes were far from complete and Mr. Yeniscavich asked if I could work on the shoes over the next weeks. It took four days in the class, working a few hours each session to finish the shoes. I told Papa what I was doing at school and Solomon and Moses told me they were doing the same thing, making a pair of shoes in class. I knew then this was the way Mr. Yeniscavich introduced us to the school and had shoes made for three boys that needed them.

Mr. and Mrs. Popolinski were very wonderful people. They were an older couple that never had children. She was about 70 years old and Mr. Popolinski was about 75 years old. They even had a barn where we could keep our horses. I think we made her nervous, she was not used to having children in the house. Mama and Papa had a bed, Gueti and Rosa had a bed and we boys had a bed. I had never been in a house with four beds. Mama and Mrs. Popolinski cooked and the girls cleaned. In just a few days, Mrs. Pololinski said it was very nice to have us in the house and we were becoming the family she never had.

The first week in Odessa was wonderful. Rabbi Kautzman got permission to take the whole family on a tour of the city after school but Papa stayed in the shoe shop. He had been to Odessa many times and knew Solomon, Moses and me were anxious to see the sights. Rabbi Blatt gave us his carriage and we drove around Odessa. There were buildings five and six stories tall and I had never seen such tall buildings. There were wonderful stores in Odessa. Mama made the comment the women wore dresses different than in Roshen. The Rabbi said the women of Odessa always had the latest fashions from Paris, but they were the Christian women in town. The best part of the tour was the electric streetcars. That first day became imbedded in my memory but that night I thought of Roshen and was saddened as I lay in the bed in the dark. The sadness disappeared the next day because we rode a streetcar. Words cannot explain the exhilaration of an eleven year old boy from a small village on his first streetcar ride in his life.

After our tour, Rabbi Blatt told us to be careful because we were not in Roshen any longer. He warned us not to go outside the Jewish area alone because there were bad sections of town. I had never thought a town having a Jewish area or a bad section. In Roshen, everyone was a neighbor of everyone else. He explained there were sections of town as bad as Sodom and Gomorrah. I wondered if they were that bad why God didn't destroy them. That night at the Popolinski's, Papa spoke to all of us children about wandering off in such a large city. He said the tour we had should be enough. We always obeyed Papa and there was no reason not to follow his instructions. We toured the whole city that week after school and it was exciting and I think it even helped take Mama's mind off leaving Roshen, for a short while anyway.

The Rabbi explained that there had been pogroms against the Jews in Odessa in the past. He said the main pogroms were in 1821, 1859, 1871 and 1881. The Jews controlled the wheat exports from Odessa and the pogroms were from rivals that wanted to take over the exports. After each pogrom, Odessa always settled down.

That week flew by and the Sabbath was here. I was really going to attend a real synagogue! Friday dragged by so slow and finally we arrived home from school and Papa was already home from the shoe shop. The Popolinski's lived about ten blocks from the synagogue. We were ready and instead of walking, we were riding. I felt just like the Czar as he rode through Roshen on that bear hunt. People were already at the synagogue when we arrived. Moses had not had his Bar Mitzvah and had to sit with the women. I spent most of the time looking at the inside of the synagogue, the windows and memorials around the walls. I wanted to read the memorials but I wasn't too good at reading yet but I was learning fast.

Papa would not allow work on the Sabbath. Mama and Mrs. Popolinski did not cook and we couldn't harness the horses for another tour of Odessa. Several people came to the house and the plight of the Jews was a main topic. The Jews had been scattered around the world and I had even had my nose broken by Christians, but that was the only problem I had ever had. Palestine was mentioned and Rabbi Blatt wanted to visit before he died. Turkey owned Palestine and Jews were not permitted to enter Palestine, but I didn't pay attention.

Sunday morning was just as fascinating as the Sabbath. All the bells in the churches began ringing. I had heard the bells during the week but not like Sunday morning. All the bells were ringing and it was a harmony of sounds. I recalled the single bell in the church in Roshen, but nothing like these bells. I could hear one bell that must have been very large because it rang with a deep bass tone. Solomon,

Moses and I sat in the front window and listened to the sound then just as soon as the bells started, they stopped. Mrs. Popolinski explained that most of the people in Odessa were Christian and I knew they went to church on Sunday morning.

Papa took us boys to the waterfront to watch the ships arrive, unload and then leave. He knew we would go to the waterfront sometime and he thought it best if he went with us. Alexis, a boy from the school went with us because he was more familiar with the waterfront. Papa warned us about the dangerous of the waterfront. I had never seen so much water in my life. The Black Sea stretched as far as the eye could see and I had never seen so flat a horizon as this. There was more water here than the Dnieper at high flood. The ships of the Black Sea Fleet were huge and were owned by Mr. Terekoff, a Jew from Odessa. Papa explained the main cargo of the ships was wheat from the Ukraine and was delivered all over Europe. There were warehouses along the waterfront and I watched a constant stream of men carrying bags of wheat from the warehouse up the gangplank onto the ship. They walked to the hold, dropped the bag and walked off another gangplank to pick up another bag. I asked Papa how much the bags weighed and he told me they weighed about 80 pounds. The workers reminded me of a line of ants. There was a whole line of ships along the docks and they were all being loaded with wheat from the warehouses. I had seen wagons loaded with the bags being delivered to the warehouses. Alexis had told me the bags contained wheat and were stored in the warehouses until they were loaded on ships.

I watched a crane unloading wooden crates in a cargo net. I asked Papa what was in the crates and he said they could contain anything from farm machinery to glassware, items people or shops had ordered. When the cargo net was full, a crane from the ship, picked up the net and it was lowered into the hold of the ship. Alexis explained all the activity on the ships. We saw passengers boarding several of the ships and he said they were Christian pilgrims going Palestine to visit Jerusalem. I had heard of Jerusalem all my life and here were people actually going there. We spent several hours at the waterfront and I watched one ship pull away and get smaller and smaller as it approached the horizon.

We had been in Odessa for three months and Papa came home with a pleasant look on his face. It had been a long time since I had seen that look on his face. Roshen was still alive in my memory but it was beginning to fade. The street, houses and people were not as vivid as they had been. Papa greeted Mama with his traditional kiss on her cheek, he then greeted the Popolinski's, then us children. I couldn't tell whether Papa was getting used to Odessa and his memories were fading as mine were. I knew Mama still had vivid memories of Roshen, I heard her crying several times when she didn't know I was near. She placed her oil lamp on a shelf in the parlor and I can recall that she would look at it one time and her face glowed, then the next time her face was sad. I always wondered what she was thinking when she looked at her oil lamp.

Papa had some good news. Mr. Shipirski had three daughters and all were married and none of his sons-in-law were shoemakers. He told Papa he wanted to retire and move to Moscow where two of his daughters and grandchildren lived. He asked Papa if he would take over the shoe shop and Papa agreed immediately. He apologized to Mama that he hadn't consulted her first but she said it was a good decision. The shop had a good business and Papa had met many of the customers. The boys worked in the shop when we were not in school. Papa said the school came first, that we could always work in the shoe shop, but we needed to have an education. Some of the boys from the school would stop by the shoe shop while we were working and we had made many good friends in Odessa.

Odessa was a good city and I had trouble understanding what Rabbi Blatt said about the bad sections of town.

The Shipirski's had owned the shoe shop and lived above it for almost 50 years and I knew it had to be sad for them to leave the shop, Odessa and all of their friends. Mr. and Mrs. Popolinski lived about ten blocks from the shop and while we were moving out, Mrs. Popolinski said she was going to miss us. She had become the grandmother I never had. Mama said she would check on them and she did.

The business improved in the shop. As long as Papa didn't own the shop, he wasn't able to thrust his personality in the foreground. Papa never met a stranger. On many days, instead of working in the back of the shop, he took a small bench and worked in front of the store and talked to people as they walked by and brought many new customers into the shop. I wanted to work in front of the shop like Papa but we were never allowed. I wanted to work in front because you could watch the people pass by, watch the electric cars and the sound of the wheels on the cobblestones. My job in the shop was to make the bottom of the boot and shoe. Papa did all the stitching on the shoes for the customers. He did all the stitching by hand in Roshen and had a stitching machine in the shop in Odessa but never let us boys use that machine. Papa still made us boys stitch pieces of leather together just to ensure we were proficient. I had stitched shoes in Roshen, but I think Papa didn't trust that stitching machine and was afraid one of us boys would get hurt. Papa didn't seem too protective, but when he was he could be overprotective.

Mr. Terekoff came to the shop one day. He had seen Papa working on a pair of boots and came to talk. He asked Papa if he could make a good waterproof boot. Papa told him he could make a very good waterproof boot. Papa walked into the shop and brought out a jar of tallow. Papa explained how he used the tallow on the leather to make it waterproof and last longer. Mr. Terekoff left and in just a short while brought an old pair of boots for Papa to repair. He asked Papa to make a new pair of boots, using the old pair as a model and make them waterproof. Papa began working immediately on the boots and in less than a week they were finished and Mr. Terekoff picked them up when he returned to Odessa. The next day Mr. Terekoff returned to the shop and was praising the boots and said they were the best waterproof boots he had ever worn. Papa explained that the rains in the Ukraine demanded a good waterproof boot.

Mr. Terekoff became a permanent customer of Papa's and made a contract with Papa to make boots for the whole Black Sea Fleet. He owned twelve ships with fourteen crew members on each ship. This was 168 pairs of waterproof boots. Papa talked to the three of us. He said he was going to have to hire another man to help make the boots if Moses and I didn't think we could handle the work. It was decided that I had enough schooling and began to work in the shop full time. Solomon and Moses continued their education and worked in the shop part time. My job was to deliver the boots to the sailors of the ships. Mr. Terekoff gave Papa an itinerary of the Black Sea Fleet, when the different ships would be in Odessa. When a ship came in, I went to the docks and picked up the boots to be repaired. When the ship returned, I took the repaired boots and picked up more boots to be repaired. Moses made a very good boot and I will say he made a better boot than I did so it fell to me to deliver and pick up the boots at the docks. This increased Papa's business and he added a note to his letterhead when he sent out his statements, "Boot Maker to the Black Sea Fleet".

I wondered why Papa hadn't included Solomon in work in the shop, then I was told the reason. He was going to America. Uncle Herman, Mama's brother, had contacted the family in America and wanted to sponsor Solomon. He lived in a place called Dallas, Texas, and had changed his name from Shmukler to Golden. He said Golden sounded more American. He had a shop and wanted to bring Solomon over to help since he and my aunt had no children. He prepared the paperwork, sent the money, and Solomon was ready to go to America. I wanted to go also and thought I should have been chosen since I was the oldest, but it was not to be. In April of 1902, we put Solomon on the train for Germany to leave Bremerhaven for America. I asked why he didn't leave from Odessa and Papa said no one could leave Russia from Odessa, that Germany was the best place to leave. Mama, Rosa and Gueti cried and I felt like I was losing a brother but Solomon said we would all be together very soon. The train left and there was emptiness in the house and shop. We did get letters from Solomon and Uncle Herman and it seemed life in America was wonderful.

Mr. Terekoff brought Captain Sergei Malikofsky to the shop. He was the captain of one of Mr. Terekoff's ships and his right-hand man. He would be the point of contact for delivering the boots to be repaired and picking up the repaired boots. Sergei explained that he was busy but would have a person to deliver and pick up the boots. We then went to the waterfront and Mr. Terekoff explained to the customs officials the plan for repairing the boots. The customs office was a busy place and I would be a hindrance to their operations with the boots being delivered and picked up. Mr. Terekoff knew all the customs officials and explained that I would be picking up boots to be repaired and delivering the finished boots back to the ships. He told Papa he wanted me to go with him to the docks and Papa agreed. We walked to the Primorsky Stairs, which I had seen many times. These stairs were almost a hundred years old and went down to the water. There were 200 steps and I was glad I wouldn't have to make this trip every day. I was introduced to Mr. Karbosky who was in charge of the customs office and a friend of Mr. Terekoff. It was explained what I would be doing and Mr. Terekoff and said it would not be a problem for me to pick up and deliver the boots.

I became acquainted with many of the sailors on the ships in the Black Sea Fleet and they began telling me stories of Greece, Italy, France and other ports in Europe. Athens, Naples, Tripoli and Haifa were ports they visited but were just names to me. My imagination was running wild, to meet people who had been to these places. This whetted my appetite and I wanted to see and visit these places. I wanted to travel. I had already seen a good portion of the world and I wanted to see the rest. It was becoming clear there was a world of difference between Roshen and Odessa. Delivering boots to the waterfront became routine. I had a pushcart in which I delivered the boots to the waterfront. All the workers in the customs office knew Papa, Moses and me and we were never stopped, just waved on through to deliver our boots.

Customers came to the shop and would sit and talk to Papa. He would tell them about Roshen and how his shoe business struggled in such a small town where few people used money. I would think of those simpler times

The Primorsky Stairs

and did have boyhood memories of Roshen, but I enjoyed Odessa. I looked at the lamps along the street in Odessa and Roshen didn't have one streetlight. I was growing up and approaching my twelfth birthday and that meant my Bar Mitzvah.

Mama and Papa both prepared. Mama had three women to help cook the food and Papa was telling about how our home in Roshen served as the Synagogue. The moment arrived. We went to the synagogue and Rabbi Blatt greeted me as a man, not a boy. Papa was beaming and his chest stuck out and I wanted to make him proud. I was allowed to read from the Torah for the first time and had trouble with the pointer but I was very nervous. After the service, we ate and drank and the men toasted me! I would now be able to sit with the men. I saw a tear in Mama's eyes and I think Papa's eyes were even moist but it was difficult for Papa to cry. Papa told me I would now have a larger responsibility in the shop.

I became adept in making the latest fashion on women's shoes and Moses continued making the boots. Women would bring me a photograph of the latest footwear from Paris and asked if would make them a pair. We kept the measurements of the customers on file, but I always measured their feet to make a new pair because I always told them that people's feet change. Papa's shop had a good reputation and many Gentiles became customers. Many very fine looking young ladies came to the shop and I was pleased to talk with them. Before long, Papa would be a wealthy man. I mentioned this one time and he told me he was the wealthiest man in the world with his family and friends. He continued that money did not buy happiness.

Alexis and I became fast friends. He was born and raised in Odessa and knew the city like the back of his hand. One thing did surprise Alexis. As we walked along the waterfront, many of the crew members of the Black Sea Fleet called out my name and I returned their greeting. I told Alexis that I made boots for many of the men from the ships. I went with him and he showed me the special sights of Odessa. He knew most of the beggars on the waterfront and they were really nice people and even many of them lived around the buildings on the waterfront. He took me around the old section of town. Odessa had been a Turkish city and the old section was hundreds of years old with stone buildings and narrow twisting streets. He told me about the caves where the stone had been quarried by the Turks to build the old section of town.

The caves were about two miles from Odessa and were along the cliffs of the Black Sea. Hundreds of years of quarrying limestone had created large caverns along the coast. The cliffs were honeycombed with those caves and Alexis had been in every one of them. We spent the rest of the day in the caves and many days afterward, talking about subjects that only two young boys that are coming into manhood can. I had no idea how important those caves would be in the near future.

Chapter Four
The Jewish Self Defense League

Odessa was good for a young Jew. The world came to our port and I spent as much time as I could watching the ships. When I took the boots to the ships, I always spent more time than needed, just looking at the ships at the docks and wondered what cities they had visited. I think Papa knew that Moses had a greater interest in the shoe shop than I did, although I could make a good boot and shoe. I heard Mama tell Papa that I was the restless type and she knew Roshen couldn't hold me and didn't think Odessa could hold me either.

Papa's business grew and his reputation grew along with his business. He gave money to the poor, money to all three Synagogues and even to the Catholic Sisters who ran the orphanage in town. Papa, Moses and me each had our own special customers. We each knew just how they wanted their boots and shoes made. Papa was good to Moses and to me and the days passed and I was growing up. I was entering my 17th year.

There was rattling of swords on the horizon. Japan and Russia were in a dispute over the ownership of Manchuria. The Czar was building the Trans-Siberian Railroad. The work was good for many people, except for most of the workers on the railroad and the cost was bankrupting the country. Stories circulated about working conditions on the railroad and the number of deaths in laying the track. Japan wanted Manchuria because they had very few natural resources in their islands. Manchuria was rich in resources and Japan wanted this area and was prepared to go to war. The railroad was a common topic in the shop. War clouds were gathering and Mama was concerned. The government asked for volunteers for the Army and then conscription began. Many young men in Odessa joined and many others were conscripted.

It was reported that many advisors to the Czar told him to take the money for the railroad and build a new Navy. Most of the ships in the Russian Navy were old and outdated. I had seen our ships in Odessa and they were impressive. War broke out and it was swift and deadly. The Japanese captured Port Arthur and our Navy was sailing around Africa to Japan to take Port Arthur back. It took weeks for our Navy to arrive and the battle was short and decisive.

Our ships were some of the largest in the world and were considered invincible and that was their downfall. The Japanese had newer, smaller ships, which were faster and could maneuver around our ships. The Japanese under Admiral Heihachiro Togo destroyed everyone one of our ships except the flagship of Admiral Stephan Makarov, and on the return to Russia, he committed suicide. The war was over and we had lost. Many a fine young Russian had given his life for the Czar. I'm sure many Japanese also were killed for their Emperor and I never understood what the war was about.

The war news saddened everyone. Papa said no one wins in a war and there was plenty of room for everyone and we should try to get along with the other counties. Odessa was in mourning. Being a seaport, many young men joined the Navy and were killed in the war with Japan. There were several young men from the Synagogue that joined and were killed in the war and Christians and Jews were both asking why.

Alexis and I went to the waterfront because there was always something exciting going on, and to get away from the talk of the war. There was a commotion along the waterfront. The ship Potemkin was in port and word spread of a mutiny. We heard the officers on the Potemkin had executed a sailor for some offense and the crew had mutinied and killed several of the officers. A group of soldiers were approaching the docks and we found a safe place where we could watch. The mutiny on the Potemkin as well as the people of Odessa were demanding to know why we lost the war with Japan. There was no appeasing the families who had lost brothers and sons. The soldiers came to the waterfront to keep the peace but a revolution almost started.

My whole family attended the funerals and memorial services for the young men in Odessa, Christian and Jew. It was now a common sight to see veterans of the war on the streets of Odessa. Some were missing an arm or a leg and Alexis saw these veterans mainly on the waterfront in the bars. They had turned to alcohol to try to get away from the memories.

People were demanding why a small country like Japan could have defeated Russia, one of the most powerful nations in the world. Alexis decided the Russian military was overconfident. Japan was a small island but had a newer and better Navy. If the money spent on the Trans-Siberian Railroad had been spent on the military, we wouldn't have lost the war. Revolution was in the air, the war was lost and the Potemkin was in mutiny.

Leonoid Verikoff was one of Papa's best customers. He was in the shop and heard a rumor that was circulating. He heard that Jews in the Russian Army and Navy had given our secrets to the Japanese and that some of the Jews had deserted and joined the Japanese. Papa said that was ridiculous. Many a young Jew had been killed in the war and we were loyal to the Czar. I agreed with Papa and refused to believe the rumor and the Russian people wouldn't believe the rumors either.

Before the pogrom, a Jewish French Army officer had been tried and convicted of treason for giving military secrets to the Germans. He was accused of being a traitor and sent to Devil's Island off the coast of South America. After this trial, Theodore Hessel organized the Zionist movement in Austria. He knew the trail of Dreyfus, the French officer, was an attempt to destroy the Jews worldwide. There was even a movement in the Zionist Organization to find a home for the Jews. Some wanted to go back to Israel, which was owned by Turkey and some wanted to go to Uganda in Africa, which was owned by England but this was all before the pogrom in Odessa.

I was delivering several pair of boots to Captain Sergey Malikofsky. He was the captain of one the ships in the Black Sea Fleet. On the way to the waterfront, a man yelled an insult at me and said that I was the reason his son had been killed. I told him that I had friends killed in the war and the rumor about the Jews was ridiculous. He yelled the Jews would pay for what we had done. I was upset. I didn't enjoy having people upset at me. I gave the boots to Captain Malikofsky and I told him what happened and he said he had been hearing rumors all morning and he thought trouble was brewing. As I was leaving he told me to be careful. He was also a Jew and I could see the concern in his face. The last thing he told me was that we must remain strong and convince the people the rumors were not true.

During the next few days, some of Papa's oldest and best customers picked up their boots and shoes and then said they would not be back. They said they would not do business with a Jew. Papa tried to explain that the rumors were false and he told them that Jews had been killed in the war. Papa told me it was impossible to talk to people when they have a closed mind. The business in the shop fell off and people didn't stop and talk like they used to. What hurt Papa were the insults hurled at Mama when she went shopping. The Rabbi told everyone to make sure they went out in a group, not to go out alone in public. I was worried. Odessa had been good but the city was changing.

Kishinev, the capitol of Moldvaia was northwest of Odessa. About 50,000 Jews lived In Kishinev which was about half of the total population. The Great Synagogue was built in 1818 and by 1900 there were 16 Jewish schools in Kishinev. Jews, employing thousands of Jewish workers, owned more than half of the factories and printing houses. Kishinev was becoming a hotbed and an anti-Semitic campaign began with the backing of the Minister of the Interior, Von Plehve. The movement was published in the newspaper in Kishinev, *Bessarabets*. The movement became virulent when the body of a Christian child was found and a Christian woman committed suicide in a Jewish Hospital. The pogrom started on April 6th, 1903 just after Easter and we heard it was led by a Catholic Priest and lasted for two days. Local students, seminary students and local Russians and Romanians killed 49 Jews and wounded more than 500. More than 600 Jewish businesses and shops were looted. There was a garrison of 5,000 soldiers stationed in Kishinev and they took no action to stop the pogrom. The second pogrom occurred on October 19th, 1905. Nineteen Jews were killed and 56 injured[1].

Thousands of Jews left Kishinev and the economic life of the city stopped. After each pogrom, Papa with a group of Jews went to Kishinev to help clean up and bury the dead. Moses and I ran the shop and each time when Papa returned, he told Moses and me horror stories of Kishinev. He was worried that if it could happen in Kishinev, it could happen in Odessa. I wondered why the people didn't think of the Jews that died fighting along with the non-Jews during the war with Japan. Many of Papa's customers stopped coming to the shop. Some told Papa they knew the truth about the rumors but didn't dare come to the shop because they had been threatened if they continued doing business with a Jew.

On the Sabbath, the Rabbi talked of the dead in Kishinev

---

[1]Nahum Goldman Museum

and the situation in Odessa. The Rabbi talked but gave no solutions. I knew it was only a matter of time before the pogroms started in Odessa. There was a man from Odessa who came to the Synagogue by the name of Vladimir Jabotinsky. He was one of the organizers of the Zionist movement in Russia and changed his first name to Ze'ev from Vladimir. Ze'ev is Hebrew for wolf. He said we had to organize a Self-Defense. The Anti-Jewish movement was growing in Odessa. I had hope the movement would settle down until I witnessed a group of people breaking windows in a Jewish bakery while the Cossacks watched. The Cossacks were the police force and carried a long sharpened pole on horseback. They were to keep order but they stood and watched the crowd. I knew if the Cossacks stood and watched, we had no one to turn to.

Papa, Moses and I began taking boots to Captain Ma-

This is a photograph of Ze'ev Jabotinsky.

likofsky. We didn't go anywhere alone now. I told Papa we had to do something and he told me "Two wrongs do not make a right." I told him that to defend ourselves was not wrong. He told me the shop had not been damaged the bakery had been repaired. The Captain met us, took the boots and told Papa he had German lugars and ammunition on his ships if we needed them. Papa did not believe in guns and told the Captain there was another way. I wondered what Papa was thinking after he had seen the horror of the two pogroms in Kishinev.

The captain shrugged his shoulders and walked off. We returned to the shop and found both windows broken. Mama and the girls were upstairs but were unhurt. Papa was angry but he forgave the people that broke the windows. He grabbed a broom and began sweeping the glass and said everything will return to normal. For the first time in my life I talked back to Papa. I told him he was crazy. He looked at me and I saw the hurt in his eyes. I also saw his strength but that strength was not going to keep the city of Odessa from destroying us.

I talked to Mr. Jabotinsky and agreed with him that something had to be done. I told him about Captain Malikofsky and the lugars and ammunition and that I was returning to the waterfront. Against Papa's warning, I returned to the waterfront and Captain Malikofsky's ship was still there. I told him what had happened and his eyes were full of anger. I told him I wanted to buy the lugars and ammunition for the Hagannah that was being organized. He looked at me with his steel gray eyes and said the weapons were for defense only and told me to go home. I returned to Jabotinsky and we talked more. The next day we returned to the waterfront and talked to the captain. Jabotinsky was almost 30 years old and had a cooler head than I did. I was only 17 years old and brash. The two talked and they agreed the Self Defense should have weapons.

The captain came to the Synagogue and said he could smuggle the lugars and ammunition into us but we had to pay him in advance. He said the method of delivery would be in the boots brought to shore to be repaired. He explained that if we were caught, we would be executed as revolutionaries. Before he left the Synagogue he had the money in hand. Members in the community donated money when they were informed of the plan for the Self Defense. We had to be very careful who we talked to. We had to ensure word of the Self Defense did not leave the community because the Russian Police force and the Cossacks would attack in force and they had proven in the past they did not and would not protect the Jewish community. He then told me no one else knew what we were doing for our own safety. He said if we were caught, besides being shot, the ships would be confiscated and Mr. Terekoff would also be shot and he had no knowledge of the plan. The plan was extremely dangerous but also exhilarating. I felt like I was doing something worthwhile.

The captain left and said he would return in five days and told me that I had to meet him at the waterfront, not Papa and not Moses. I informed Mr. Zabiltilsky that I was picking up the boots in five days and we agreed we would meet at the Synagogue. The five days passed and I took my pushcart loaded with repaired boots to the waterfront. On the waterfront, waiting for me was Captain Malikofsky with six pairs of boots in a small cart. He had never brought boots ashore. He always had someone else deliver the boots to me. He stared a hole through me and said we would exchange boots on Sunday, and it had to be Sunday. Most of the Russians would be in church and there would not be a full crew at the Customs Office and not to break my normal routine. He then told me not to look in the boots because that would only call attention to the boots and me. I put the boots in my cart and went back through customs. I waved to the officials, they waved back and I returned to the shop. That return trip to the shop was one of the longest trips in my life. A Cossack passed and gave me the "once over" and went on his way. I arrived at the shop and pushed the cart to the back of the shop where my worktable was located.

The boots the crew members of the Black Sea Fleet wore resembled a Cavalry Boot. They were tall and came above the knee in the front and below the knee in the back. This protected the knee while they worked on the ships. I looked in a boot and there was a German luger pushed down into the foot section. In another boot was about 50 rounds of ammunition and two extra clips. Three boots had a luger and the other three had ammunition inside them. I put the boots on the floor as I normally did and Papa looked up from his table and said, "The boot business is very good." I agreed and wondered how to get the lugars and ammunition out of the boots because Papa had no idea of the plan. I knew he would not agree with what I was doing but I felt it was necessary.

The shop door opened and the bell rang and Papa went to the front. I quickly took out the lugars and ammunition and put them under a pile of leather. The problem now was to get the weapons and ammunition to Mr. Jabotinsky and out of the shop without Papa knowing. It was my lucky day because the man that came in the shop wanted Papa to come to his home and measure his wife's feet for a new pair of shoes. She had trouble walking and normal shoes hurt her feet, so Papa left with him. I put the weapons and ammunition on the pushcart and piled leather on top. It was not unusual for Papa or me to push the cart piled with leather, so it would raise no suspicion. I pushed the cart to the Synagogue, entered the gate and Mr. Jabotinsky was waiting for me just inside the gate. An iron fence, eight feet tall surrounded the Synagogue and the grounds. We went between the Synagogue and school and I explained how the weapons and ammunition were delivered. He seemed pleased and said this is what we needed. He then informed me that forty-five young men had joined the Self Defense. Mr. Jabotinsky was a born leader and the driving force behind the Self Defense.

We agreed to hide everything in the caves near the bluffs. There was no chance of being discovered in the Synagogue because it was one of the few places where we could have privacy because the outside world never came in, but we felt it was not proper to hide the weapons there. Three more members of the Self Defense joined us and we each took a luger and ammunition and hid them in our pockets. No other member of the Self Defense was informed of how the weapons and ammunition were being smuggled in. This was done in case one was picked up, he would have no information where they came from. We left the Synagogue alone and met at the caves two hours later. If we were to leave in a group, it might have called attention to us. Alexis knew the caves and found a remote area to hide the weapons. Jabotinsky further explained that we had to know how to fire the weapons, that they were useless unless we knew how to fire them.

Moses helped me take the boots to the waterfront. He told me he was afraid of being caught. Sergei told us again that if we were caught, it meant being shot, the ships confiscated and the shop burned. Everything depended on how level headed and calm we remained. In three weeks, each member of the Self Defense had a luger and ammunition. I smuggled in one extra weapon and ammunition and hid them in the stone wall around the back of the shop. I located a stone in the wall, loosened the mortar and removed the stone. I was able to hide the weapon and ammunition behind the stone. I wanted to have a weapon at the shop in case of an emergency.

I was not spending as much time in the shop with Papa. I was meeting the Self Defense in the caves to learn to fire the luger. I retrieved my weapon from the stone wall and told Papa I had to leave the shop and he told me to be very careful. He pointed at my shirt and I could see the outline of the pistol grip of the luger. He knew what we were doing all along. He may not have agreed with us but he didn't try to stop us. The only thing he said was that I had put the family, the shop and the Synagogue in danger. I didn't tell him anything so he would have no knowledge of the Self Defense, but I think he knew anyway. There seemed to be a sadness in his face. He was against violence and here I was going to the caves to learn to fire a weapon.

The caves were perfect for our use. As we learned to fire the lugars, the shots could not be heard outside the caves. In Russia a citizen could not have a weapon, especially a Jew. Mr. Jabotinsky knew how to fire the luger. He had lived in St. Petersburg and studied electricity and joined a club sanctioned by the government where they learned to fire weapons. He was well acquainted in St. Petersburg and had many good contacts but he could not use them for the Self Defense because we were outlaws in the eyes of the government.

Jabotinsky instructed each of us in the proper use of the luger and he always emphasized safety. After he instructed each one of us, we were on our own to fire the weapon. We set up targets in the caves and we were becoming proficient. Not all of us could meet in the caves at one time. We gathered in groups of three or four. There was always a chance of drawing attention if we were in a large group and it was safer in smaller numbers. Jabotinsky always told us to never draw attention to ourselves. He said if one was captured, it would mean the end of the Self Defense, our death, the death of our families and no telling what else. As in the past, there were always jealous Russians waiting to jump on, use and take away a livelihood for themselves.

I recall the time when Zabilisky was in the caves with four of us practicing with the luger. He stated we were very good but then he said there was a whole world of difference between shooting a target and shooting a human being. I heard what he said but didn't pay much attention to it. My anger was growing for the people of Odessa and the Self Defense was allowing me to channel that anger. The thought of the Self Defense had an air of excitement about it. Being seventeen, I was young and foolish. If I were caught I would be shot as a Revolutionary, only after being tortured and interrogated. Would I be able to withstand the tortures? Would I inform on Jabotinsky and the other members? If other members were caught, would they inform on me? I had never had to face death before and I didn't know if I would recognize him. I don't think I realized the Self Defense was laughing in the face of death but he was also laughing back at us.

The Self Defense met at the Synagogue soon after on the Sabbath. This was a time we could move without drawing attention. Instead of attending services, we met to devise a plan of action. Jabotinsky said it was impossible to protect the entire Jewish section of Odessa but we could protect the three Synagogues. Odessa had the Central, Brodsky and the

The Brodsky Synagogue in Odessa

other Synagogues, which I can't remember the name right now. With the 45 members, we split into three groups of 15 each to go to each Synagogue. We identified who would go to which Synagogue. My family attended the Brodsky Synagogue and I requested that. Other members requested the Synagogues their families attended. A few had to join in groups where their families did not attend, but we needed 15 at each Synagogue. Jabotinsky and Lexis were both at the Brodsky Synagogue. All three Synagogues had an iron fence eight feet tall that surrounded the temple, buildings and courtyards. The iron posts in the fence were sharpened at the top and this always kept intruders out.

After the family returned home, Papa asked why I wasn't in the service. I talked to him and told him that if the time ever came and I asked him to take the family to the Synagogue to please not ask any questions but to go immediately. He stared at me with a seriousness I had never seen before then he agreed. I realized for the first time in my life I was telling Papa what to do and it scared me. Papa was a wise old man and I was only seventeen years old.

We told the Rabbi in each Synagogue of our plan. I don't they agreed but we explained that the pogroms in Kishinev were not going to happen in Odessa. I still don't think they agreed but said they would not try to stop us. We didn't inform anyone else of the plan but we did tell the families of the Self Defense that if asked, they should come to their Synagogue without question. The next several days, we smuggled the lugars and ammunition into the Synagogues. The Rabbis were not happy with us bringing weapons into a place of worship but the memory of Kishinev was still sharp in their minds. I realized there were thousands of Jews with no idea of what was going to happen and had no warning as our families did. If too many people became aware of our actions around the Synagogues, it could cause trouble. I was despondent about the people that had no warning and what might happen to them.

On the appointed day, Moses and I took several pairs of boots to the waterfront that we had repaired. It appeared that everything had returned to normal. We were not smuggling guns anymore and there was nothing to hide. We went by the customs office and approached the ship. Sergei came down the gangplank with two crew members and gave us several pairs of boots to be repaired and took the repaired boots. He gave me an envelope with payment that I was to give to Papa. He then told Moses and me to be careful that the Cossacks were now watching the waterfront. They were looking for weapons being smuggled in. I had to smile to myself and think, "They are too late." We had nothing to hide, but we heeded the warning. We left the dock and approached the customs area and we saw two Cossacks on horseback. We pushed the empty cart past them and they sneered at us from atop their horses. They were watching all the Jews.

Jabotinsky worked for the City of Odessa as an electrician. He was well respected for his knowledge learned while in St. Petersburg, but he was still a Jew. The next Sabbath, he told me that he had been hearing rumors flying around where he worked. There was talk of reprisals against the Jews for the war with Japan. He said weapons were good but if a large mob appeared, we would be in trouble. I had never known him to be worried but now he seemed troubled. I began to doubt if we could save the Synagogues or even our families. A new plan had to be devised.

Odessa had streetcars that ran on the overhead electric lines. The technology of the streetcars had been brought to Odessa from Belgium and were the first electric streetcars in Russia. He continued to tell us that several other Jews worked with him at the Electrical Department. He had taken a chance and talked to several of them and they agreed to help. At night, they would loosen the overhead electric lines in front of the Synagogues and when the time came, the lines could be lowered to the pavement to help protect the Synagogues. If nothing happened, the lines could be re-attached. Over the next several nights he worked with the other Jews that were electricians and loosened the lines. I stood guard with other members of the Self Defense as lookouts for the Cossacks or anyone else that might discover our plan. One night I carried the tools for Jabotinsky and his electric gloves. I had never seen such a pair of gloves. They allowed him to work with electricity without being hurt, but I knew nothing of electricity or how it worked.

Everything was ready. The weapons were in the Synagogues, the electric wires had been loosened and we had our pre-determined positions, but could I kill another human being?

Chapter Five
The Pogroms

The morning was calm. Mama commented that I had
been absent a lot from home and the shop lately. I couldn't
tell her what I was doing. Papa knew but he didn't tell
either. Mama was always the worrier for the family. Papa
told her that I was seventeen years old and needed time to
myself. His comments were welcome but did little to relieve
Mama's worries. I had a bandage on my arm and Mama
asked what had happened. I had never lied to Mama and
Papa and I couldn't lie now. I told them I had a tattoo. Jewish law forbad tattoos and Papa stared at me but didn't say
anything. I took off the bandage and showed them what
I had done. I had a Magen David inside a heart. Around
the heart were the Latin characters that read, "If I am not

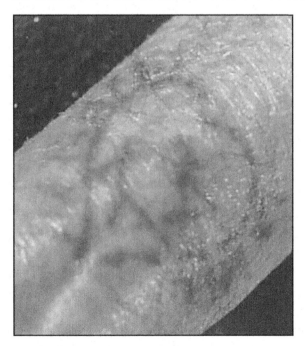

This is the photograph of my tattoo.

for myself, who will be?" This became the motto of the Self Defense. Papa returned to his breakfast, Mama had a look of anguish on her face and Moses was curious. Alexis and me had tattooed each other with a needle and bottle of ink. We had to use the Latin characters. If we used Hebrew, the Russians would have become suspicious and if we used Russian characters, the Russians would have able to read it. In Hebrew, the motto read, "Eem Ayn Anee Lee Mee Lee." I call the tattoo self pride which is not a very good virtue but I wanted to show the world that I believed in the Self Defense.

Mama was pregnant again and Papa told me not to upset her. Upsetting Mama was the last thing I wanted to do but the situation demanded that we protect ourselves. Breakfast was over and Mama and Rosa were doing the dishes when there was a hurried knock at the door. It was not the usual knock of a neighbor, it was a frightened knock. Papa opened the door and Mr. and Mrs. Kautzman rushed in. Mr. Kautzman had fear in his face and Mrs. Kautzman had been crying. I knew the pogrom had started. Mr. Kautzman said a crowd of about 40 or 50 people were breaking windows in the neighborhood and as they walked down the street, more joined. Both were talking and said the crowds were shouting insults at the Jews and that we were responsible for the death of their family members and for Russia losing the war.

I told Papa to take the family and go to the Synagogue immediately. I looked him straight in the face, not as a son, but as a Jew trying to protect other Jews. He nodded in agreement and told Mama to gather a few things. I told Papa we didn't have much time. Rosa and Gueti were asking what was going on. Papa took over because I had to leave but I made him promise to go to the Synagogue immediately because if they didn't it could mean their lives. As I was walking out the door, I heard him tell Mama to forget getting any things because they had to leave now.

Mama didn't move as fast because she was expecting and was worried about the child she was carrying. I was going down the street and just turning the corner when I saw the family and the Kautzman's come out the door. I walked at a hurried pace but not too fast to draw attention. I saw several Cossacks on horseback and saw a pall rising over the Jewish section of the city. The burning had begun and the Cossacks began drifting toward the fires. This gave me a chance to hurry.

There was already a group of people at the Synagogue, family members of the Self Defense. Jabotinsky was there directing people over the live electric wires on the ground. He yelled at me and said he had the wires down in front on two Synagogues and one to go. He told me take over the job as getting the people safely over the wires and not to touch them because it meant instant death. I began pointing to the wires and he took off like a wild animal and prayed to God that he didn't meet any Cossacks. A steady stream of people was coming to the Synagogue. All of Odessa had stopped. The electric street cars had stopped and word of the pogrom spread like wildfire. An eternity passed, then I saw the family approaching. Mama was carrying a satchel and being helped by Mrs. Kautzman. Rosa was walking with Papa with Mr. Kautzman and Gueti came behind. I helped Mama over the wire with her satchel, then Mrs. Kautzman, Rosa and Gueti. Papa and Mr. Kautzman were with the last people to enter the gate and it was closed. The women and children were taken inside the Synagogue and the men were outside with the Self Defense. I stood with Papa and several men were talking about the rioters breaking into the Jewish homes, looting, ransacking and raping. One man lowered his head and began to cry softly and another man embraced him.

Jabotinsky returned and we opened the gate. The smoke over the city had become darker and we could hear the shouts of the rioters, mixed with the screams of the Jews as they broke into their homes. We heard breaking glass and splintering wood. The rioters didn't have weapons so no shots were heard. My blood was boiling. How could Russians do this to other Russians? The crowd turned a corner and came into view of the Synagogue. They were like a frightened herd of cattle following the leader. I could see the distortion on their faces as they approached. They didn't look human, more like demons, which in reality they had become. The crowd carried clubs and some were covered with blood. The Synagogue gates had been opened to let in a few more Jews then quickly closed. The crowd approached the gate and it grew in size. People were joining the pogrom from all directions. I could see them kicking in doors of the Jewish homes and it was well orchestrated. They did not bother the homes of Non-Jews, they knew where we lived. I could hear the screams of the injured and the dying and I screamed with them.

The fifteen Self Defense members stationed ourselves at regular intervals inside the fence, our pistols at the ready. I had a magazine in the luger and my pocked were stuffed with additional magazines filled with ammunition. I had about 200 rounds in magazines and an additional 300 loose rounds. Moses walked up behind me. He spoke and I could hear the fear in his voice but I was just as afraid as he was. He asked, "How long have you had the pistol?" I said, "Long enough." Papa then walked up beside me and put his hand on my shoulder and said he was proud of me. Tears welled up in my eyes because I didn't know what was going to happen. He then said, "It is a sin to murder, but you have to protect the Synagogue first, then the people." I couldn't believe what he had just said. I knew the people were more important to me but to Papa, the Synagogue was a symbol that must be protected. He then said, "I have been worried about your recent actions, but I know now they were worthwhile." He then left and joined Mama inside the Synagogue. I was again struck by the fact that I was only seventeen years old but had been telling Mama and Papa what to do all morning. I had ordered Papa and he had followed everything I had said.

The crowd was about 100 feet from the fence and shouting anti-Jewish insults at us. I recognized several of Papa's customers and knew how ugly the pogrom was and was going to get much uglier. How many people had been killed already and would we be able to save the Synagogue and ourselves? I saw the Cossacks on their horses behind the rioters, watching the whole situation and they were doing nothing to stop the riot. The crowd was intent on burning the Synagogue because to them it was the center of deceit and cooperation with the Japanese that cost the lives of their sons, brothers, husbands and fathers. The crowd had centered on the gate and all fifteen of the Self Defense were now at the gate. Clubs and clinched fists were raised and the crowd rushed the gate. Jabotinsky screamed about the live electric wires on the ground but no one heard him. Sixty feet separated the wires from the gate and I heard the pop of the electricity and screams. I saw clothes burning and people writhing in their death throes and the smell of burning flesh. That is a smell that I carry with me to this day. The crowd stampeded over the dead and the dying and was intent on breaking down the gate. A shot rang out and we all began firing. I fired at a man rushing toward me, the bullet hit him and threw him into the people behind him and they stomped over his body. If the bullet didn't kill him the crowd did.

Shooting a human is not like shooting a target just as Jabotinsky said. When I pulled the trigger and saw the man fall, I got violently sick. Alexis grabbed me and jerked me to my feet. "Get sick later, we don't have time!" he screamed at me. The rioters were still coming. I emptied my magazine, pulled it out and inserted another one and continued firing. Only this time, I didn't aim, none of us were aiming. Dozens of rioters dropped, dead and dying.

The crowd suddenly stopped as it had started and began to run away. Someone yelled, "Stop firing!" When the firing stopped, the crowd turned and slowly approached the gate with hate in their faces. The electricity had been turned off at the main station and the wires were no longer protection for us.

An eternity passed as we faced the rioters and they faced us. I looked at the other Members of the Self Defense and the shadow of the bars in the gate fell on their faces. Hate was on both sides of the gate now. The Cossacks were still on horseback watching the whole incident and still did nothing to stop the riot. The crowd began to mill with an occasional insult. They were restless and would rush the gate in an instant if not for our weapons. My mind reeled as I wondered who was dead and who was dying and whose home had been burned? Would our ammunition hold out and if it didn't what would happen to us? Had we signed our own death warrant?

A group of soldiers approached. Finally, the Army was coming to our rescue. To my horror, I saw the soldiers speak to the Cossacks then ride off. They were going to do nothing to help us. The Cossacks began to disperse the crowd. They rode into them and told them to go home. There were grumbling about the Cossacks helping the Jews but everyone had to obey the Cossacks. They were the police force and could and would kill anyone for any reason. One man threw an insult at one of the Cossacks and it was his last words. The Cossack rode at him full force and impaled him on a spear. The spear went completely through the man. The Cossack then placed his foot on the body and pushed him off his spear. The limp body fell to the ground. The crowd passed the body with the same numbness I felt. The only people to stop were his family. They were weeping openly and looked at the Cossack as he turned and rode off with an air on insolence.

The crowd was dropping clubs and burned out torches.

Some threw them down in disgust. I vomited again when I thought about the human lives I had taken. I wanted to have a sense of accomplishment that we saved the Synagogue but at what price? I felt that I had driven a permanent wedge between the Jews and non-Jews in Odessa. A Cossack rode up to the gate and said, "Stay inside if you want to be safe," then sneered as he rode off. I thought, why do the people hate us? We didn't lose the war. Jews had been killed in the war. We were made a scapegoat to preserve the political system.

It was late afternoon, the crowd was gone but a haze still hung over the city. The Cossacks and soldiers patrolled the streets. I had a hatred for both. They could have stopped the pogrom but didn't. The Cossacks had no loyalty to anyone except their own and I couldn't understand why the Army let the pogrom continue. As long as the Army patrolled the streets, we knew it was safe to leave the Synagogue. Our first concern was who was alive and who was dead. How many lives had been taken? Jabotinsky saw my anger and said, "We have taken lives also." I turned and faced him, "How can you compare the lives we took to protect our families with the actions of the rioters with their random murdering and pillaging?" He said, "Killing is killing and is forbidden." I told him, "Murder is forbidden, what we did was not murder." I didn't want to hear his logic, I wanted a target for my anger.

Alexis stayed with the people in the Synagogue and Jabotinsky and me along with several other Self Defense members went out the gate. The gate slammed shut behind us. It rang with a noise that I had heard many times before but this time it was different, it echoed my anger. The first Jewish houses we came to were next to the Synagogue and had been protected but a few blocks away we found the first burned out houses. The doors had been splintered, windows smashed and walls broken. I entered that first house cautious because I didn't know what I was going to see. The body of a man lay in the first room. His head had been bludgeoned to a pulp and blood was splattered on the walls. The bodies of his family were in the back room and blood was everywhere. Everyone had been beaten to death with clubs. The man's wife naked body was on the floor and I didn't even want to think what had happened to her. I heaved because I had nothing left to vomit. Other Self Defense members appeared and frustration and hatred filled the air. Curses were whispered because the Cossacks were in the streets watching our movements. We were powerless to do anything. Any action on our part would only cause more death and destruction. The only thing we had to be thankful for was the Army patrolling the streets. If the Army was not there, I don't know what the Cossacks would have done to us.

The crowd didn't return and the people left the Synagogues and everyone began helping. All wounds were cared for. A lost look or blank stare was met with a hug from the nearest person and children were held by strangers. Even some non-Jews came and offered to help. They told us they were incensed at what happened. We thanked them very politely but the climate of the city we didn't think they should be helping us because of the anger of the rioters might turn on them. None left and they asked what they could do to help. We told them they could move debris and that we had to remove the dead and wounded. This worked very well and helped to ease my anger that not all the people of Odessa hated us. The dead were brought to the Brodsky Synagogue. According to the law, we had to wash the body and prepare it for burial, but there was no time. There were too many dead. We had to bury them for health reasons. Husbands brought the bodies of their wives and women brought the bodies of their children and it was a sight I shall never forget.

Alexis and I were with a group of people searching burned and pillaged homes for bodies three blocks from

Papa's shop. I entered a house and furniture and belongings were strewn everywhere. In one of the rooms, I saw the arm of a doll protruding from under a pile of clothes. I picked up the arm and stood there in shocked silence. It was the arm of a child that had been torn from her body. My anger silenced my scream. Alexis walked into the room and saw me holding the arm. I wanted to recoil in horror, but I had seen too much horror and too many lives snuffed out. We both searched the room and found her other body parts. She had been literally torn limb from limb. I found her torso and she was a girl less than a year old. She had long brown hair that circled her face, which looked like the face of an angel. Her death became agony for all of us. What monsters could have done this, ripping her life out as they tore her body apart? This wasn't the people of Odessa that I had known. I carried her body out of the house and brought it to the Synagogue. A group followed me because in an instant she had become a symbol. The mourners increased and more bodies were brought to the Synagogue. In all about 400 Jews had been killed. We couldn't follow the law, all we could do was dig a trench in the cemetery and bury them in a mass grave. We dug a grave and put twenty five bodies in each grave. There was no way we could identify the bodies because most had been burned. We vowed a monument would be erected and they would not be forgotten. How can people do that call themselves Christian.

Countless lives had been shattered by the riots. I heard husbands and fathers weep as they told how they were forced to watch as their wives and daughters were repeatedly raped. Women watched as their husbands were bludgeoned to death and children wailed in horror as they saw their parents killed. Hatred had spawned hatred and the whole city was a tinderbox that could explode again. What type of people could have done this? They couldn't be human. We were taught to love and honor each other but what happened in Odessa? The world was full of hate and that hate had been turned against us and I couldn't understand why.

This is a photo of some of the dead from the Pogrom in Odessa.

This is just one shop in Odessa destroyed in the Pogrom. There were hundreds of shops that looked just like this one. I got these photos from the Russian Archives.

Chapter Six
The Black Sea Fleet

Odessa would never return to normal. The glass had been shattered in the widows of Papa's shop but it had not been burned. Many other store owners were not as lucky Other stores had been looted then gutted by fire. Papa was having the glass in the windows replaced and Moses and I were cleaning. After several days, the shop was almost back in working order when Mama's time was due. It was the only ray of sunshine through the entire ordeal. So many killed and a new life was to come into the world soon after such carnage.

Simon Abrahamevich Kerbel was born soon after the pogrom. I was 17 years old when he was born and Moses was 15 years old. Several people came to the house to congratulate Mama and Papa. Under normal circumstances there would have been a houseful of people, women to help Mama and men to celebrate with Papa. This time Rosa and Gueti did all the work. The people that did not come to the house were trying to put their lives back together or helping friends get their lives together.

It was good to have a baby in the house. Simon became a symbol also. That little girl with the brown hair I found in the house after the pogrom was the symbol of destruction and Simon was the symbol of rebirth. Papa's business was back in operation and many new customers came along with the old. A lot of the new customers not only came for shoes but to see Simon. Some of the old non-Jewish customers returned. They came in silence, not knowing what to say and not knowing how they would be received. One man started to tell Papa how bad he felt and Papa put up his hand and said it was better not to bring up the past. Some new customers came that were not Jews and told Papa they didn't agree with what happened. Papa just smiled and said it was in the past.

I directed my anger in making a better boot and shoe, but something was missing from my work. My heart was just not in my leather work. I spent more time at the waterfront when taking boots to the sailors. I had a longing when I watched the ships leave the docks and I found myself wanting to be on one of the ships. I was ready to leave Odessa and wanted to forget what happened here. But I knew I would carry the horror of the pogrom as long as I lived, but I had to get away. Mama's brother, Herman, had gone to America several years ago and I thought about going there but he had already sponsored Solomon and I didn't think he would sponsor another Kerbel boy.

Sergei met me on the dock on one of his return trips and in the course of our conversation mentioned that he needed a fireman and was having trouble finding someone qualified. I suspected he might have told me for a reason because I had talked to him that I wanted to get away from Odessa and the memories of the pogrom. On the way back to the shop I decided to tell Papa that I wanted to take the job. I would be pulling up all my roots and starting a new life and I think I needed this. My whole world had been turned upside down by the pogroms. I had watched people die and know I caused some of the deaths.

Papa knew I was the restless type. I had been working in his shop for almost seven years. I told Papa that I wanted to take the job on the ship. He told me that he knew I was troubled by what happened and all of the violence in the pogrom. He then told me he heard my nightmares every night and that he was not against my taking the job on the ship. He then told me Mama was not in favor. She voiced her opinion very strongly that I should not take the job but should stay in Odessa. Solomon was gone and she didn't want to lose another son. I told her that she hadn't lost Solomon and Moses could take over my work in the shop and I just had to get away. She then stated that through everything that had happened recently, she felt like she had lost Solomon. Mama was always the strong one in the family but Papa said he would talk to her. Papa was a wise man and knew I had to get away.

Several days passed and Papa and I were working when he stopped what he was doing and asked if I were ready to give up our dietary laws. Without hesitation I said I was. It told me he knew that I was going to take the job with or without his permission. He said he wanted me to be sure that I knew what I was doing. I put down the shoe I was working on and turned to face Papa. I told him that after we had been in Odessa for a while, I had become accustomed to the big city and Papa's shoe shop, but seeing the rage and hate in the faces of the people during the pogrom made me realize how small Odessa was and I needed to get away. Papa said he was not going to stop me. He then said it was difficult to let go of a son who he had watched grow from infancy through childhood in Roshen then forced into manhood in an adult world with so much hate. He then told me that I had saved the entire family, that if I had not taken over, the whole family would have been murdered. I did not want to hear that. I had always depended on Mama and Papa and to think they depended on me made me nervous. He did say it was sad when Solomon left and it would be sad when I left.

Papa and I had never talked so long and when we finished, I ran to the waterfront. I searched the docks for Sergei's ship but it wasn't in. I was informed he would return in seven days. That was the slowest week of my life. Work in the shop, conversations with customers and even the streetcars dragged by. Odessa was trying to return to normal. Most of the old customers had returned and stated a vast injustice had been done. Some wanted to raise money for reparations but many people said it should just be forgotten. I just wanted to get away.

That week passed and I went to the waterfront. I hoped Sergei's ship would be in. I stood on the dock and saw Sergei's ship on the horizon and the closer the ship came to the waterfront, the more nervous I was. Was the job still available? Would I be able to leave Odessa? Thoughts raced through my mind and they were all about leaving Odessa and getting away from the memory of the pogrom. Two tugs met the ship and brought it to the dock. Crew members on the ship threw the lines to workers on the dock and they tied them to the docking quays. It was almost more than I could stand. I had to talk to Sergei as soon as possible. I saw him against the rail with some passengers on the ship and he waved. I waved but did not want to appear overly excited. The gangplank was pushed up to the ship and the passengers began debarking. The ship had about 30 passengers and I counted everyone as they left the ship. After the passengers, some crew members came off and finally Sergei came down. He walked up to me and we shook hands. I told him that I wanted to take the job if it was still available. He informed me he was holding the job for me because he had talked to Papa several weeks ago and Papa told him that I wanted to leave and wouldn't stand in my way. Sergei told me that Papa loved me very much and said I should be very thankful for having such wonderful parents. I was relieved the job was still available. I told him things had begun to settle down in Odessa but the memory of the pogrom was still boiling and the memory of that little girl was in my nightmares every night.

The ship was leaving as soon as the next load was on board. Sergei gave me a list of the items I would need. He told me to go home, get the items, say my goodbye's and return to begin my job. I returned to the shop, walked up to Papa and said, "Papa, I love you." He was hammering on a boot, stopped and looked at me. "You talked to Sergei," and that was all he said. Papa never showed emotion but from that day I carried Papa in a special place in my heart.

He sat his hammer down and said, "A man does not give another man advice unless it is asked for." I said, "Papa, give me some advice." He said, "You are a man now, but still my son." He said he was looking out for my best interests and we talked for several hours. He told me to obey the law, first God's law then the law of man. He told me I would be visiting many cities and to remember the Sabbath and visit a Synagogue. He then told me if there was not a Synagogue to visit a church because people were talking about God in the churches. He warned me away from the saloons and people that lived on or near the waterfront in cities I would be visiting. He then told me that I must forgive. Rumors and mistrust can make bitter enemies out of friends and that we must rise above the pogroms. I can say that I really tried to follow his advice and obeyed him and his advice did me well. I told him that I would be returning to Odessa on a regular schedule. He told me this is what he told Mama, that I would be returning to Odessa.

I returned to the harbor. The air was fresher, the sun was brighter and even the seagulls seemed happier. The world had a different view and I was happy. Sergei brought me on board and showed me my quarters. I was to share a room with four other crew members. He told me to put my things away and report to the deck for duty. I put my bag on one of the bunks and returned to the deck. Wheat was being brought from a warehouse on the waterfront. The wheat was in the 80-pound bags Alexis had told me about and were being stacked on the docks by workers from the warehouse. The crew of the ship was bringing the bags on board. I was handed a collar that fit across the shoulders and the bag of wheat rested on that collar. There were two workers that lifted a bag of wheat and set it on the collar. I joined the line of about seventy crew members taking the bags onto the ship. The first few bags were fairly easy then they became heavier. We carried the bags onto the ship on one gangplank and set them down next to the open hold, then walked off the ship on another gangplank to pick up another bag. I was informed that about three thousand bags of wheat would be put in the holds. I saw the quarters on the ship and wondered how all seventy men carrying the bags onto the ship had rooms. I was told before we left the docks that Sergei hired workers to help bring the bags on board. If the crew members filled the holds, we would be too exhausted to stoke the boilers. I remember one dockworker that brought the bags out of the warehouse. I always tried to be near him because he sang as he worked. His name was Fyodor and I knew him from Papa's shop but didn't know he sang. He had a deep bass voice and it resonated as he worked. I looked forward to returning to Odessa to see the family and hear Fyodor sing. One day, he was gone. It seems a man from Germany had heard him sing and convinced him to come to Germany and he became an opera singer. I never saw Fyodor again and often wondered what happened to him.

ANMS1092[175]

This is the type of passenger and cargo ship sailing in the Black Sea Fleet.

The other crew members were in better shape than me and I wasn't able to keep up the pace in loading and unloading the bags. I had been working an hour or so and Sergei told me to go below and help stoke the boilers to get the ship ready to leave. Leonoid was also a Fireman and took me to the boiler room. The boilers were in the bottom of the ship and were about eight feet in diameter. I was taught how to stand in front of the boiler and throw in a shovel of coal. We worked two hours on then had four hours off. Two hours was all a body could stand in front of the boilers when the fires were burning. We worked the boilers for twenty four hours then were off twenty four hours. Leonoid told me I should use the 24 hours I was off to rest.

The ship's hold was filled, the gangplanks removed and we were ready to leave. Sergei came below and called me up on deck. I went up, my face blackened with coal dust and saw Mama and Papa on the dock. Mama had a handkerchief over her nose and Papa was waving as the dock receded. I waved back and told Sergei I had to return to work and went back below. If I hadn't left then I might have started crying and everyone knows that a man doesn't cry.

I couldn't believe I was leaving Odessa. I had never seen so much water in my life. I had never been on water where I could not see land. After my first two-hour shift on the boilers, I went up on deck and watched the ocean. Standing on the deck, I saw large fish in the water swimming along with the ship. Papa told me everything in the world was one of God's miracles and I knew this was one. I spent about two hours on deck and then went to my quarters to get a little rest the remaining two hours before I returned to the boilers. I no more than laid down and I someone shaking me. It was time to go back on duty. I didn't realize how tired I was from loading the wheat and stoking the boilers.

I recall the first meal on the ship. This was the first non-Kosher meal I had ever eaten. I did not know what to expect. It was the evening meal and was a bowl of stew with bread and cheese but we could eat all we wanted. The stew was good as was the bread. I had watched the cook preparing the meal and saw him cut meat with a knife then cut a piece of cheese with the same knife. This would never have happened in Mama's kitchen.

The first stop was Greece. Leonoid and I were on deck as we approached Athens. Sergei barked orders and we had to go below to prepare to unload bags of wheat. There was a list attached to the wall in the hold and it listed how many bags of wheat were to be unloaded at each city. Four hundred bags would be unloaded at Athens. I was excited as I carried the bags up from the hold. I was actually at the docks in Athens. One crew member was in the hold and counted the bags as I helped load them into the cargo net. The net and crane could handle twenty five bags. The crane then lifted the net and lowered it onto the dock. Sergei was on the dock talking to the man that accepted the wheat for the government.

After the four hundred bags were unloaded, I was on deck with Leonoid. He pointed to a hill and said that was the Acropolis. I asked what the Acropolis was and he explained the Parthenon and what it meant to the Greek people. I stared at the Acropolis and couldn't believe I was seeing it. We then unloaded wheat in Sicily, Italy and France. Our last stop was at Jaffa in Palestine. Jaffa was not a deep water port and a small boat came out to the ship and twenty pilgrims who had sailed with us climbed down into the boat to visit the Holy Land. Leonoid told me that if the small boat wasn't available from the shore, we would row the pilgrims to shore in one of our boats. We didn't pick up pilgrims returning to Odessa and we left. I watched the coast of Palestine disappear and remembered what Rabbi Blatt said about wanting to visit Palestine before he died.

That first trip was magical even though the work was hard. I couldn't believe that a boy from Roshen was seeing the world. The ship returned to Odessa but didn't pull up to the docks We dropped anchor out in the bay because the docks were filled with other ships in the Black Sea Fleet. They were doing the same as my ship, loading wheat and pilgrims. A boat was lowered to take crew members to shore and Sergei told me to be back at the ship in two days to prepare for the next trip. I ran from the ship to papa's shop. I entered and grabbed him and hugged him. I told him that I missed the family but it was good to be away from Odessa. He took me into the house and Mama kissed me on the cheek and asked how long I could stay. I told her I could stay two days then had to leave for the next trip. Moses asked where I had been and I explained the Parthenon, Sicily, Italy and France and Palestine. Papa then said he would like to visit Palestine also to see where our people came from.

The trips around the Mediterranean became routine. I had looked on the Acropolis many times and never thought of it as mundane but it did become mundane along with Mount Vesuvius at Naples and St. Mark's Square in Venice. I was always a little jealous of the pilgrims that came on board. They were going on a pilgrimage to Palestine and I wanted to go with them. I was fascinated about going to Palestine because of the stories I had heard and read about in the school in Odessa. We had about 20 pilgrims on each trip. Sometimes we stopped at Palestine first and sometimes we unloaded wheat around the Mediterranean then went to Palestine.

Taking pilgrims to Palestine was a way the Black Sea Fleet made a profit. I had been working with the Black Sea Fleet for almost two years and was making money. Every time we returned to Odessa, I visited with the family and gave Papa a little money. He said he was putting the money away for me when I returned to Odessa. He told me that I couldn't work on the ships my whole life. I thought about what he said and knew I could never return to Odessa, the memories were still there and the little girl was still in my nightmares even though they were not as numerous now.

We returned to Odessa and I spent two days with the family then returned to the ship. We loaded the wheat and the pilgrims and headed out. We unloaded wheat at Naples, Genoa, Monaco and Marseilles. We then headed toward Palestine. The main business in Jaffa were the pilgrims. We anchored offshore but the small boat did not come out from Jaffa. Sergei told us to get our boat ready. The ship had taken pilgrims to shore on several occasions but I had never gone. The crew members that rowed the pilgrims to shore had to clean up. Sergei asked if I wanted to help row the pilgrims to shore this time. I was ready. I went to my quarters and cleaned up as fast as I could and returned as the boat was being lowered. I went with three other crew members down in the ship to a door that opened just above the water level. The door was opened and the four of us stepped into the boat then helped the pilgrims into the boat with their luggage. All twenty pilgrims would fit into one boat and we began rowing. I was put in the front of the boat because the two crew members in the back guided the boat. The three other men had rowed pilgrims to shore many times and I used my experience on Papa's log raft to help me row. The boats were about 30 feet long and took about thirty minutes to row to shore. The pilgrims got out of the boat and a man informed us that some pilgrims would be returning on our ship, but would not be ready for about thirty minutes to an hour. We picked up the pilgrims, returned to the ship and headed back to Odessa.

We spent two days in Odessa then loaded the ship with wheat and pilgrims and headed out. I decided on this trip, I was going to get off and see Palestine, if we rowed the pilgrims to shore. If the small boat came out from Jaffa, I would have to wait until the next time we rowed to shore. I became a regular oarsman on the boats because I was able to handle the boats very well due to my experience on Papa's rafts. We unloaded our wheat around the Mediterranean and headed toward Jaffa. I was lucky, the boat did not come out from Jaffa. Leonoid was an oarsman on this trip. I told him I was going to get off and see Palestine. He said I couldn't go ashore. I had seen other crew members go ashore and I was going. I told him I wouldn't be gone long. I got off with the pilgrims to see Palestine and I followed the group to a small building. I had taken a shower and put on clean closes and even combed my hair.

Palestine at that time belonged to Turkey and we were met by Turkish officials that spoke Russian. One official keep looking at me and when I got to the desk he asked my name and my business. I told him "Louis Kerbel and I wanted to see Palestine." Even though I had clean clothes on, I wasn't dressed as the other pilgrims. I had my work clothes on, but they were clean. A Turkish official asked, "Are you a Jew?" I said "Yes" and to my surprise I was arrested. I was returned to the boat and two officials got in to go to the ship and talk to the captain. They informed Sergei what I had done and he was furious with me. The Turks left and Sergei turned to me and I could see the rage in his face. "Why did you go ashore? You know Jews can't go to Palestine!" I told him that I didn't know I couldn't go to Palestine because no one told me I couldn't go. Sergei had become like a father to me and I'm sure Papa told him to look after me. He said, "Turkey owns Palestine and Jews cannot go to Palestine!" I told him, "No one ever told me Jews could not go to Palestine." He told me that I would be taken off his ship when we returned to Odessa and he was very upset because I was a good worker and also he didn't know what was going to happen.

We docked at Odessa and sure enough there were several soldiers waiting for me at the dock. I was arrested and as I was being led away I could see the sadness in Sergei's face. I was taken to the local magistrate and was informed as punishment I would serve two years in the Army of the Czar. I didn't think that was so bad, I was afraid I was going to be shipped off to Siberia or something happen to Mama and Papa. I was not allowed to visit the family and I was worried what might happen to them. The soldiers put me on the train with other conscripts to be sent to Kiev for Basic Training in the Army of the Czar.

I barely slept a wink on the train. We had no sleeping compartments and I didn't know what to expect but I was relieved and worried at the same time. I was worried the government might start watching the family and relieved that I knew what my punishment was to be. I wasn't too unhappy.

The trip to Kiev was uneventful. The countryside rolled by and it reminded me of the land around Roshen. I thought of the old house and the people in Roshen and memories began to flood back and I felt a longing for Roshen when life was so much more simple and easy. I began to feel uneasy that I was to be in the Army the Czar, the same people that stood by and watched the people of Odessa kill the Jews in the pogrom. The trip took three days and I pondered my position those three days. The train pulled into Kiev and I was taken to the Kaserne. I noticed as we walked, I saw only German officers, I saw no Russian officers. I was processed with the other conscripts. We were issued uniforms and taken to the barracks. It was late afternoon and we had to clean the barracks, which took most of the night, and then and told training would begin in the morning.

Chapter Seven
Army of the Czar

I think we barely got to sleep when we had to get up to start training. A man entered the barracks and shouted for all of us to get up. I can't repeat the exact words he used but he called us some names I had never heard before. I was still groggy and not sure what to expect. Orders were barked for us to get outside and fall into formation. There were about 50 new soldiers and none of us knew what a formation was, but the sergeant informed us very quickly what to do. Although I didn't have much education, the experience of serving on the Black Sea Fleet served me well. The crew members of the Black Sea Fleet were expected to act as professionals on one of the Czar's ships. I knew what the sergeant wanted but most of the new recruits had trouble understanding what the sergeant wanted them to do, so I would explain his commands to the others. I did this until he came and stood in front of me and screamed if he or I were in charge of the formation. Of course I answered that he was and I was trying to help. He assured me he didn't need any help and for me to keep my mouth shut. That was my introduction to the military.

The uniform I was issued didn't fit but no one else had a uniform that fit either. The sergeant walked back and forth in front of our formation like a banty rooster, barking orders and telling us what we were to do and what we were not to do. If someone moved or did something, he would hit them, and hard. I couldn't understand why he was hitting us and I didn't remember half of what he said, so I decided I was going to watch what the others did. If they got into trouble, I was not going to follow them. If they did not get into trouble, I would follow suite. It generally worked. I was interrogated about getting off the ship in Palestine and I explained and explained. I was informed my two years was punishment and would not be easy. I had scrubbed the floors in Papa's shop but never like I had to scrub the floors in the barracks. I didn't mind scrubbing the floors if they needed to be scrubbed. I would be working on the floor then a sergeant would walk in with mud on his boots then kick me because there was mud on the floor. I didn't dare talk back because I was the lowest rank and I was a Jew. I worked in the mess hall and was put on every detail that came along. I had to do all the details, wash my uniforms, work in the kitchen and scrub floors. Army life was beginning to be miserable and when I didn't do something correct or just when they wanted, I was hit.

We were taken to the building where we had breakfast except I wasn't permitted to eat as the beginning of my punishment. We were farmed to different areas and I was sent to the leather shop in the artillery unit. Sergeant Mischikoff told me that since I was a shoemaker, I would be good at repairing the harnesses for the horses that pulled the caissons for the artillery. I met Private Mallikoff in the tack room. He was in charge of all the tack for the unit and it was my job to repair what he decided needed repairing. There was a pile of halter and bridles on a table that needed repairing. I had a lot of experience in working in leather and it was easy, easier than making boots and shoes but I missed the Black Sea Fleet. I was used to traveling the Mediterranean and the tack shop was an awfully small place.

Private Mallikoff barked "Attention" and a Captain walked into the shop. I wasn't accustomed to military life and didn't stand up. Mallikoff yelled at me, "When an officer enters, stand up!" I quickly stood up and the Captain walked up to me. He said, " I understand this is your first day?" I told him it was my second. He then said, "The next time I didn't stand up when he came in, it would be my last day." He mentioned that I had gotten off in Palestine and I was a Jew and had been arrested. His name was Captain Helmut Heit, a German officer. I didn't understand why the military used German officers and not Russian officers. Germany and Russia had not traditionally been friends. The wife of the Czar was German and she adopted Russia and converted to the Russian Church but using German officers to train Russian soldiers was beyond my comprehension.

Captain Heit spoke to Private Mallikoff then spoke to me. He said that he understood I was a shoemaker. I told him my grandfather was a shoemaker, my father was a shoemaker and I was a shoemaker. He wanted to know how good I was because a good boot maker was hard to find. I told him I could make a good pair of boots if he could get the leather. He left and in about an hour a soldier appeared with an old pair of boots that belonged to the Captain along with a large piece of leather. Between working on the harnesses, scrubbing floors and other details, I made a pair of boots, using the old boots as a pattern. I finished the boots and they were taken to the Captain. The next day he came to the tack shop. I snapped to when he walked in and he said, "I have never worn a pair of boots as comfortable as these." It was like a miracle, all the details stopped. I had no more floors to scrub and no more pots and pans to wash in the kitchen. Mallikoff told me that he heard the Captain tell the Sergeant to ease up on me. In a few days, a pair of women's shoes were brought in with a piece of leather. I was informed the shoes belonged to the Captain's wife and wanted me to make a pair of shoes for her. Before long I was making shoes for the Captain's whole family and Army life became easy. Then a horse was assigned to me. I groomed him, made new harnesses that wouldn't rub him and he became my best friend in the Army. His name was Peter, after Peter the Great. Whoever trained him was good because he knew the Army commands better than I did. In a few months I was doing less work on the harnesses and making boots for the Sergeants and their families. My duties did not include making the boots and shoes and was not paid for my work, but it made Army life a whole lot easier. The Captain brought in a pair of boots, which was unusual, he always had someone bring the boots and he talked to me personally. He told me these boots were for the Colonel and he wanted to give them as a gift. He told me they had to be the best pair of boots I had ever made. I finished the boots and they were taken away and I never heard another word about them. Another boy, Josef, was brought into the tack shop to work on the harnesses and I spent more time making boots and shoes.

Josef was local, from Kiev where we were based and we became friends but he knew I was a Jew and whenever anyone else was around, he was less friendly toward me. Our artillery unit went on maneuvers in the country and on parades to larger cities to include Chernobyl, Smolensk and once even to Volgagrad. Field maneuvers and parades always meant repairing the harnesses, cinches and whatever else needed fixing. I always helped Josef after the maneuvers and I know he wanted to become better friends but I understood the way he felt. I didn't mix well with most of the unit members. A lot of them were from small towns, uneducated and had been conscripted. They didn't want to be in the military and they drank and chased easy women than drank more until they passed out. Being in the military was not easy

I remember the day we had pistol training. Sergeant Petrofsky was instructing us in the use of the pistol. We trained with the Russian Pistol and were in formation. Petrofsky was going from man to man, instructing how to use the pistol. None of us had ever handled a weapon before and he was in front of a soldier next to me. I can't remember that soldier's name now but Petrofsky was doing something incorrect. Captain Heit was watching the training and had his luger out. He walked up to the Petrofsky and instead of placing his luger back in its holster, he handed it to me then began correcting Petrofsky. I was very familiar with the luger from the Self-Defense.

Without even pausing and from habit, I removed the clip from the luger, cleared the weapon and replaced the clip in a matter of a few seconds. The Captain glanced at me and instantly I knew I had made a mistake because none of us had handled a pistol, especially a German Luger. When the Captain had corrected Petrofsky, he retrieved his luger and walked away. Petrofsky was in front of me, instructing how to use the Russian Pistol. I never heard a word he said. I heard, "Kerbel, are you paying attention?" I straightened up and watched how to use the pistol. I knew my life was over. Any member of the Self-Defense was to shot on sight. The training lasted about two hours but seemed like an eternity.

The Captain watched the whole training session, which he never did. He had better things to do than watch a bunch of Russian Soldiers in training. After the session was over and we were dismissed, Captain Heit walked up to me. "Louis, where did you say you were from?" I said, "Odessa." Then he asked, "How many did you kill?" and walked off. I knew I was to be sent to the firing squad and would be a news item, "Jewish Self-Defense Member Executed." The rest of the day was spent in terror. Not only would I be shot, but my whole family was in danger. The Captain must have noticed that I was in a state of terror and in a few days he walked up to me and said, "Louie, don't worry, I can't find anyone that can make a boot like you can." I knew that my family and me were safe.

The rest of my military career was uneventful, except for the time the Czar came to Kiev. We were notified to be in uniform and had to line the streets of Kiev. We formed up at 8:00 in the morning and lined the main road in Kiev with the people behind us. Our main duty was to protect the Czar and his family. There was unrest all across Russia and some democratic reforms had been implemented, but the Socialist movement was growing. What worried me was hearing of Jews being singled out and killed by rioters in the cities and the local police did nothing to stop it. We stood along the road in Kiev all morning waiting for the Czar and they appeared about 1:00 in the afternoon. Nicholas and Alexandria rode in a carriage with guards in front, back and both sides. They rode by, waved and rode on. It reminded me when I was a child and the Czar came to Roshen. We had been standing for five hours when they rode by. Captain Heit even made a comment. He said, "We are here to protect him and the least he could do was come to the Kaserne and talk to the soldiers.

My two years was drawing to a close. Captain Heit came to me and said, "I appreciate everything you have done." He told me I was a good soldier and hoped to see me again someday. He was returning to Germany and told me I would make a good German soldier. I realized his job was training Russian soldiers but his loyalty was with the Kaiser, not the Czar. This again made me realize that Russia lost the war with Japan because of its leadership, not because of the Jews. Most of the Germans could care less about the Russians.

I had a farewell party and the whole company was there. I had grown fond of most of the men in the company and they all had good qualities, but you had to search for those qualities sometimes. Captain Heit was there and the Colonel even made an appearance to thank me for the boots and shoes I made for his family. The Colonel was from Darmstadt, Germany, and would be leaving soon also. We sang, danced and had a good time. The party was over and I went to say farewell to my best friend in the Army. I went to the stable and entered Peter's stall. I'm sure he knew I was leaving because his back was to me. I walked up and hugged his neck then sat down on the hay. Peter lowered his head and rubbed my shoulder. I looked up and Captain Heit was there. He told me he knew I would be here and he wanted to talk to me alone. He told me I was a very unusual soldier, very intelligent, gentle and most of all, very sensitive. We had a good talk about Russia, Germany and even the Self-Defense. He told me Russia was headed for a revolution and it started with the Potemkin and the Pogroms against the Jews. We had become friends and he asked if I wanted to come to Germany. I was flattered and told him that I had an uncle and younger brother living in the United States and I wanted to go there to a place called Texas. We embraced, I saluted him and he left. I turned to Peter and told him I wanted to take him to America but that was dreaming. I laid on the hay and had a good nights sleep.

I woke up with a start. I had missed morning formation. I ran from the stable with hay hanging on my uniform and everyone was already at work. I saw Sergeant Petrofsky and repeatedly told him that I was sorry I missed formation. He said the Captain had left instructions that I was to be given the day off to prepare to leave. The Captain had indeed become a friend. I was already packed and stopped by the tack room and Mallikoff was there. We said "goodbye," each knowing we would never see each other again. I toured the company area and did my final farewells. Sergeant Petrofsky even gave me a compliment.

The date was April 28th, 1911. I had been in the Army of the Czar for two years. I was given my discharge by Captain Heit, collected my final pay which was about $3.00 and left. I was driven in a wagon to the train station where I caught the train for Odessa. As the train pulled away, I had mixed emotions. The Army provided a sense of security and I had a roof over my head and three meals a day and many men were making the military a career because of this. Ahead lay uncertainty. I could stay in the shoe shop and work but Odessa would never be the same. I couldn't return to the family because I had given up the Orthodox way of life. Solomon had moved to America with an uncle. He was Mama's brother and changed his name from Shmukler to Golden. I wanted to go to America. It had become an obsession with me.

Chapter Eight

Preparing for America

Solomon was in America, living in a city called Dallas in the state of Texas. Papa was not against me going to America but Mama was afraid if I went we would never see each other again. I knew Mama was right. If I went to America, I would never see the family again. America was on the other side of the world. My younger brother and two sisters were still at home so Mama would still have a family. She told me that when Solomon left, she knew she would never see him again and she didn't want to lose another son.

I showed Mama and Papa my Army discharge and told them that with the discharge I could get a passport. Rosa prepared supper that night. Mama was not feeling well and I knew it was due to my leaving. Papa went about his routine as if nothing was different. As he lit his pipe, he told me to go talk to Mama about America. I knocked on the bedroom door. She told me to come and I opened the door slowly and entered. She was rising from the bed and told me to sit down next to her. Without hesitation she said, "You are going to America, aren't you?" I nodded agreement and told her that Odessa was not a good place for a young Jew right now. Too much hatred had been spawned on both sides and America was a new beginning, a new life. I told her that when I was settled, Solomon and I would bring the whole family to America. She said that she and Papa were too old to start a new life. She asked my forgiveness in withholding her blessing on my trip but she was now in favor. She said how she was being very selfish in wanting to keep me in Odessa when I should be in America making lots of money and finding a young, pretty Jewish bride.

Supper that night was very relaxed and Mama talked

like a magpie. She talked how well Solomon had done in America and that I would do just as well because America was a big country and they would need lots of shoemakers. I had read Solomon's letters about the new raw, land that was available for anyone that was willing to work. He talked about the freedom the people had and that he had made many friends and most of them were Christian. He said there was no religious persecution as in Russia. After reading the letters, I wondered again why people hated us. Why couldn't Odessa be like Roshen where everyone lived in peace and respected each other?

The next morning I went to the government office and applied for my passport. The process was simple. I presented my papers to the man behind the counter. I filled out the application and he wrote down the number of my discharge and signed he had seen the discharge. The application was sent to Moscow and he told me I would get my passport in one or two months. I was 23 years old and suddenly one or two months seemed like a very long time. I told the man behind the counter that I was going to America. He said I was lucky because most people that wanted to go to America did not have passports and no papers to get one.

I wrote Solomon a letter that I had been discharged from the Army and with my discharge I could get a passport. I anxiously awaited his answer. I worked with Papa in the shop and had trouble keeping my mind on my work in anticipation of my passport arriving. The days crawled by and Papa knew I was anxious to leave. He talked more of the days in Roshen which he had never done before. Roshen was a subject that was not to be discussed. It hurt Papa more than words can describe when we left for Odessa. Mama told me how proud she was of me going to America but I knew she was sad. We had not seen Solomon since he left for America and I wondered if I would ever see my family again?

My passport finally arrived and the next day, a letter

from Solomon came. I opened the letter and Solomon told me I could stay with him in Dallas. He emphasized that I should not come to New York City. He had come through New York and Ellis Island and a quota had been placed on the number of immigrants from each country. After he got through Ellis Island, the Hebrew Immigration Service met him. They gave him a place to stay and recommended that he go west. If he stayed in New York he would probably work in a Sweat Shop above the stores in the Jewish section of town. He said the Rabbi in New York contacted a Rabbi in Dallas, Texas, and he had a job waiting for him and he never regretted leaving New York. He wrote that Galveston, Texas, did not have a quota on immigrants. They only required the immigration papers, a health inspection and money for a train ticket to the final destination. He also told me to contact Travelers Aid Society in Galveston and they would help me get to Dallas.

Money was my problem. I couldn't afford the ticket to America. No ships going to America docked in Odessa, I would have to leave through Germany. I had enough money to get from Odessa, through Poland and on to Bremerhaven, Germany, on the North Sea.

I planned every detail of my trip to America. I would travel to Germany and work in a shoe shop until I had enough money to pay my passage to America. Papa worked in the shop as if nothing was going on and Mama tried to do her normal chores around the house. The more I thought of my trip to America, the more excited I became. Every time I walked the streets of Odessa, I thought of the people that had died in the pogrom, Jew and Gentile. I couldn't stay in Odessa. I needed an outlet for my anger and hard work in a new land was just the thing I needed.

The looming trip to America gave my work in the shop new meaning. With my passport in hand and the letter from Solomon, I eagerly put every waking hour in my work. Every stitch I put in a new shoe brought me closer to my goal. The customers even noticed the new interest I was showing in the shoe business. I didn't discuss my plans with anyone outside the family and asked Mama and Papa not to either, just in case someone tried to foil my plans.

The day arrived. It was the second week of June in the year 1911. I had been packing what clothes I thought I needed but the next morning I would repack the clothes and did this several times. I finally packed my leather tools to make shoes in America. Papa finished breakfast and went to the shop as he would on any other day. Mama cleaned up without uttering a word, which was unusual. Rosa and Gueti came to my room and I think they were as excited as I was. I had only one small leather valise packed with clothes and my tools in a small package. I was ready to leave.

I walked up to Mama and she turned with tears in her eyes and said, "I now have two sons I shall never see again." I looked into her eyes and said, "Mama, I love you." The memories of Roshen came flooding back, all the small things she had done for me. Those memories would fill many lifetimes. She looked at me, kissed me on the cheek and said, "Go talk to your Papa." I walked into the shop and he continued working on a pair of boots. I stood across the table and he continued to work, "Do you have everything packed for the trip?" I said that I did that I was packed and had my ticket. He asked if I knew how to find Solomon in America and I told him that I did. He laid his needle down, looked at me and walked around the table and hugged me and said, "You are a son that any man would be proud of and you are going to have a good life in America."

Word had spread in the community that I was leaving and all morning neighbors and friends came by to say farewell. I knew I would never see my family again, my friends or see Odessa again and it felt as if part of my heart gad been ripped out and left a large hole. Midday approached and I picked up my valise and tools for the trip. Mama gave me a package for the trip she had prepared.

In the package was food, a photograph of the family and a small leather pouch. I took out the leather pouch, opened it and there was Mama's oil lamp. This lamp was Mama's prize possession and I couldn't understand why she was parting with it. "The lamp is from Roshen and will help you remember the family," she said with tears in her eyes.

The train station was six blocks from the house. I thought back about leaving Roshen and how devastating that was. This impending trip was different and I was looking forward to it. I was not being forced out because the Czar had given our land to his brother-in-law. I was going to travel half way around the world to a new land. The train was at the station and we walked through the station and I noticed there was a separate waiting area for the people on the first and second-class sections of the train. I was in the second class part of the train and I was preparing to climb on board when Mama grabbed me and gave me another hug. Rosa and Gueti both hugged me and then Papa gave me a fatherly hug and walked away. Moses then gave me a hug and I climbed aboard and gave my ticket to the conductor. Mama, Rosa and Gueti waved as Papa walked away. I removed my hat and waved back. The whistle blew and the train slowly began chugging away from the station and my old life. The family walked along with the train as it slowly began to move. Mama, Rosa and Gueti were crying. Papa and Moses were standing and showing no emotion. The speed of the train increased, the family gave one final wave. I waved back, turned, sat in my seat and I was on my way to America.

The speed of the train increased and my mind was reeling. I was on my own for the first time in my life. I was a little scared but excited at the prospects that lay ahead. We traveled north to the area from which the family had moved but nothing looked familiar. I didn't remember the land and I dozed off as the train began a rhythm on the run.

I couldn't afford a sleeper car, so I slept in my seat. For

three days I dozed, ate and looked out the window as the Ukraine passed by. I don't know how many stops we made in towns and villages to let people on and let people off. I talked to people who sat in the seats around me. Some were making trips which took years to save money to make, but most were making short trips to visit the family. I saw the carts on the roads and the children were watching the train and the boys almost always waved.

There were soldiers on the train and I began to think of the unrest growing in Russia. The conductor announced we were approaching the border with Poland. I reached into my pocket and took hold of my passport. My precious passport, my ticket out of Russia. The train stopped and Polish Soldiers boarded the train and checked papers. They looked at my passport and my ticket to Germany and there were no incidents except one soldier eyed me. This must have been a mundane job for them, checking papers on people entering Poland. We crossed into Poland with no incidents. I didn't talk to many of the people on the train except to those that spoke Russian and those that did seemed subdued. The people that got on the train in Poland seemed friendly and spoke to me and I nodded because I only knew a few words in Polish. The first class had private rooms in which to travel but no way could I afford that. I was with the masses but it seemed more alive than what I had seen of the first class passengers in Odessa. I had seen the first class people leaving their private waiting room in the station at Odessa and they were much better dressed than the masses and many of them had servants waiting on them. As in the Ukraine, the train stopped at the small towns and villages and people got on and off with packages, boxes and suitcases. I saw whole families on the train and it was a cross section of humanity.

I was in the third class of the train. The rolling hills of the Ukraine gave way to the plains of Poland. In my section of the train, I watched the children. They were so friendly and innocent, in a world all their own. One woman had a small pig strapped to her back with two children by her side. It seemed strange to have a pig strapped on her back as you would a child and wondered where she was going. The train stopped in Warsaw and most of the people got off. I saw the woman with the pig and two children walking away from the train headed for their destination. For some people, Warsaw was their destination and others just wanted to walk around the station after sitting in the seats. I was with the group that wanted to walk around. I saw families standing or sitting on their bags waiting for this train or another train headed for other destinations. I had never seen many train stations but this station was huge and I heard sounds of the people and whistles of arriving and departing trains. Warsaw had to be the largest station in Poland and the tracks went in all directions and it seemed amazing to me the trains left on time for the proper destination.

It would be easy to get lost in this mass of people, sounds and smells. I didn't walk too far. I didn't want to be left in such a large city of strangers. I wanted to see more of Warsaw but couldn't see much from the station. The train only spent about an hour or two in Warsaw and I thought back to when I had been to Poland with my father on the rafts made of logs but that was so long ago in much more innocent times. I saw people in a different part of the station getting on the cars in the first and second classes then the whistle sounded and familiar faces headed back to the train. The train slowly began moving and I was off on my trip again.

The train stopped in the towns and villages and most of the people in my part of the train had gotten off and fewer people got on as we approached the German border. We stopped at the German border and as before, our papers were checked and I had no problem with my passport. As the train slowly pulled away from the border into Germany, I thought of the Czar giving our land to the brother of his wife to hunt bear. The Czar was the cause of all of our problems. If he hadn't given our land away we wouldn't have had to move and we wouldn't have been in the pogroms in Odessa and I wouldn't be leaving Russia. Then I thought there would have still been the pogroms and I wouldn't be going to America. I was arguing with myself whether I wanted to be living in Roshen or going to America.

Poland had no natural borders and numerous armies had invaded her land and cities. As we passed through the towns and stopped at the stations, the people seemed different somehow but I didn't know why. The crowds at the stations were more organized than the towns in Russia or Poland. The smells were also different. They were not bad, but unusual to what I had smelled in the other towns. It seemed each village and city had its own signature smells and sounds. The train entered Berlin and slowed down due to the traffic. I saw horse carts and saw a cart with no horses and wondered how it was able to go. I craned my neck every time I saw one of these carts with no horse pulling it.

The train slowly pulled into the station and my first thought was how clean the station was and how well dressed the people were and how friendly everyone was. The people were different than in Odessa and Warsaw. I got off the train and walked around the station but didn't stray very far from my train. When the whistle sounded there wasn't the rush toward the train as in Odessa and Warsaw. The people slowly walked to the train and were very courteous when boarding.

Everyone found their seat, settled in and the train began moving. As we left the city, the speed increased and we headed northwest and went along the Elbe River to Hamburg. Hamburg was also a large city with a big train station and people got on and off then we pulled out for the trip to Bremerhaven. The trip was short. I got off the train and it struck me I was alone in the train station full of strangers. I was uneasy because I wasn't quite sure where to go or what to do until I saw a man holding a sign with my name written on it.

Rabbi Blatt had written Rabbi Sorenson and he was at the station holding a board with my name on it. I approached the man and he watched me as I said, "I am Louis Kerbel." He said, "I thought you were, I am Rabbi Sorenson." He took me to his home and I met his family and spent two days with them. I spoke very little German and he spoke little Russian so we communicated in Hebrew and Yiddish. We walked around the Jewish section of Bremerhaven and I met and talked with many fine people. The Rabbi took me to the Synagogue and I had never seen such a large and beautiful building. From the Synagogue, we went near the docks in the city and I was introduced to Siegfried Kellerman. Mr. Kellerman owned a shoe shop and the Rabbi had told him that I was a shoemaker in Odessa. We walked to the shop and I noticed the sign, "Kellerman Shoe Repair" over the door of a two-story brown stone building. Mr. Kellerman lived over the store and met us at the door and I had a job waiting for me. He was very friendly and needed a helper and wanted me to start right away, if I was a good shoemaker.

The Rabbi did most of the talking due to my lack of German. It was explained that I had my own tools and had made boots for the crew members of the Black Sea Fleet in Odessa. I was ready to work in the morning, but I had to have time off to attend services at the temple and was hired on the spot. We left and returned to the Rabbi's home and the next morning, I went to work for the first time in my life for someone other than my father.

I felt a little strange being in Germany, the home of the brother of the Czarina who I felt was the cause off all the family's problems. The shoe shop was within walking distance of the Rabbi's home in the Jewish section of town. Walking to the shop my first day, I stopped at the docks and watched a ship leaving. It was a ship in the North Deutch Lloyd Line and I knew I would be on one of those ships one day.

I left the house with my tools and walked to the shop. Mr. Kellerman was waiting for me and had a pair of boots to be repaired. I turned one boot over in my hands and examined it. All that was needed were new soles and heels. I opened the pouch that contained my tools and began taking the old soles and heels off. I asked Mr. Kellerman where the lasts were kept and he brought the stand with the various sizes to repair shoes. I found the one that fit the boot and began measuring for new soles and heels. It took about two hours to repair the one boot and Mr. Kellerman examined the repair. He watched me repair the boot and said, "I can tell you are an excellent boot maker and repairman."

I put all my energy in the shop to make enough money to pay my passage to America. I had prepared to rent a room near the shop but Mr. Kellerman told me I would stay with him. He didn't ask if I wanted to stay with him, he told me I was going to stay with him. Mr. Kellerman and I had trouble communicating in the beginning but I began to pick up German to talk to him and the customers. I had made waterproof boots for the Black Sea Fleet and began making boots for sailors whose ships were based at Bremerhaven. The business in the shop increased immediately and there was more business than Mr. Kellerman and I could both handle. I realized I would have the money sooner than I thought.

I met many fine people in Bremerhaven and many fine people at the Synagogue. The Self-Defense in Odessa was discussed in the Synagogue but I never joined in the discussion. I didn't take the chance of my membership in the Self-Defense being discovered. The German government may return me to Russia and that was a chance I was not going to take. When the pogroms were brought up, I said I didn't want to discuss the riots because I had many good friends killed in Odessa and it only brought up painful memories.

Mr. Kellerman closed the shop early and asked me to accompany him. We walked the street and greeted customers and came to the cemetery. He said this was a special place because his wife, Miriam was buried here. She had been dead 25 years, dying giving birth to his son who also died and both were in the cemetery. We walked to their grave and stood in silence for a few minutes then he said, "I have no one to carry on and I would like you to take over the shop." I told him I was very honored but I had to go to America. We discussed further, left the cemetery in silence and went back to the shop.

I came to work one day and Mr. Kellerman seemed apprehensive. He began making small talk then brought up my trip to America. He said again, "I want you to stay and take over the shop." He told me he had never had a worker like me before and wanted me to stay. I told him that my brother was in America and I wanted to join him. I also told him that if I was not going to America, I would have stayed in Russia with my family but I did appreciate his offer. He told me he understood because he was 60 years old and had taken the shoe shop over from his father and had watched many people board the ships to America and Canada. He then said that if he were 20 years younger he would go to America but he couldn't leave the graves of his wife and son. He said he was interested in me taking over the shop because he had no one to carry on after him. I told him he would find a young man in Bremerhaven to carry on the shop but I had to go to America. I had been in Bremerhaven almost six months and had saved almost one thousand German Marks, but it was not enough to pay for the whole trip.

I met several captains of ships in the North Deutch Lloyd Line and made waterproof boots for them and many of their crew members. I had met with Captain Edward Prehn of the ship Prinz Friedrich Wilhelm. I had seen her come to Bremerhaven then leave for the New World with her two smokestacks belching smoke and knew someday I may be on her.

In the course of our conversations, I mentioned to Captain Prehn that I had been a fireman in the Black Sea Fleet. He mentioned he needed a fireman on his ship for the next trip to America. One of his firemen had gotten married and was on his honeymoon for one week and the ship could use a replacement for that week. He knew that I wanted to go to America and told me the ship was leaving in one week and going to Boston, Miami and Galveston. I told him my destination was Galveston. I told him I had money to pay for part of my passage and asked if I could be a part-time fireman and pay for half the passage. He told me this was how many men paid their way to America and he would check with the headquarters of the ship line and let me know.

The next day Captain Prehn stopped by the shop and said I had been accepted, only because he gave me a personal recommendation and that I would be on the ship only for this trip. I had less than a week to prepare to leave. I still had four pairs of boots to finish and I had to pack and say my farewells and board the ship.

This is a post card of the Prinz Friedrich Wilhelm.

I withdrew money from the bank and went to the office of the North Deutch Lloyd Line and paid for half my fare. Captain Prehn had left instructions that I was paying for half my fare and would cover the other half in the boiler room. I finished the boots in two days and Mr. Kellerman had a sadness about him. He truly wanted me to stay and take over the shop and I had to admit it was difficult to turn down. I had become accustomed to Bremerhaven and the people and had to keep reminding myself that I was going to America. I had written letters to Solomon and he wrote back about his life in America, and if not for those letters I would have been easily convinced to stay with Mr. Kellerman. He had become a true friend and I realized true friends were rare and were to be cherished.

Mr. Kellerman had a party for me my last night in Bremerhaven. Most of the customers came by and it was a grand time. I had made so many friends at the shop and the Synagogue and I didn't know how many people had family in America. I knew it would be difficult to leave Mr. Kellerman in the morning.

The final morning came and went. I packed my clothes and my tools and Mr. Kellerman told me that I was the son he never had. At that point it would have been very easy to unpack and stay, but then I knew I had to go to America. Captain Prehn came by the shop and Mr. Kellerman grabbed me and gave me a hug that a father would give his son. It was a hug that my father had never given me and one I shall always remember. We left the shop and walked down the street and I turned and Mr. Kellerman was in the doorway looking after us. Captain Prehn said, "He is a fine gentleman." I agreed with a lump in my throat and we headed toward the bank. I withdrew what money I had left and we went to the dock. The ship was ready and we went on board and I knew many of the crew members and they chided me that I must be special because the captain hadn't escorted them on board or treated them this well when they came on board. I told them they hadn't made the captain's boots.

The quarters were in the bottom of the ship and I was given the bunk of the married crewman that left. I stored my gear and went to the boiler room and one boiler was lit to provide energy for the ship and the other firemen were preparing to light the other boilers to get the ship under way. The ship wasn't huge such as the Matsonia or Mauritana or the two new ships being built in Belfast, Ireland, which were to be the largest ships in the world. We were scheduled to leave the next morning and we were stoking the four boilers when word was passed down that I was to report on deck. I washed up first, reported on deck and there was a group of people to see me off, led by Rabbi Sorenson and Mr. Kellerman. About thirty people were on the dock and the Captain Prehn gave me permission to get off the ship and visit with them. Mr. Kellerman gave me a brand new pair of boots he had made for me. "You will need these while you are stoking the boilers," he said. I said my final farewells a second time, then boarded the ship with tears in my eyes and went back below deck.

I had watched some of the First and Second Class Passengers waiting to board the ship on their own gangplank. They were dressed much better than I was. They had much more luggage than I had and all the clothes I owned fit in one small suitcase. I wondered where these people lived and were they immigrants like me or just going on cruises to then return to Germany.

The Kaiser Wilhelm was not a new ship but a good ship. She had compartments for First and Second Class passengers but most of the people on board were immigrants going to the United States and Canada and were in steerage. The passengers were on board, the ship's whistle bellowed and the moorings were released and the ship slowly backed away from the dock. I was in the boiler room, getting acquainted with my duties and didn't see Bremerhaven disappear.

Chapter Nine
My Trip to America

My dream was coming true. It had taken almost a year to go from Odessa to the Kaiser Wilhelm, but I was on my way. This was the end of 1911 and I felt the world was my doorstep. I felt a sadness leaving Bremerhaven but not as when I left the family. I had no sadness leaving the city of Odessa, I was glad to leave, but not the family. The sadness was the family leaving Roshen and that had long been buried.

My shift in the boiler room was every other day or when I was needed. I had the upper bunk in the crew's quarters and had met all of the firemen. A boy named Helmut had the lower bunk. He had the same first name as the Captain. We shoveled coal together, ate together and talked together. He said he had a dream of going to America and owning a farm. He was saving his money to marry his girlfriend and go to America on this very ship as a first class passenger. We had our quarters different from the steerage passengers but on my day off when Helmut was working, I wandered up on our part of the deck.

I met and talked to immigrants and a large number had come from the Volga River area in Russia, but they didn't speak Russian. In our conversations, they told me their families came to Russia from German during the reign of Catherine the Great. Catherine was from Germany and invited the people to Russia with the understanding they could keep their language, culture, religion and there would be no military service. Most were Mennonite Brethren and left Germany to avoid military service. Czar Nicholas began conscripting the young men into the Army and a mass migration began to the United States and Canada to avoid military service. Many of them had family members in the areas around Hastings, Nebraska, Lehigh, Kansas, and

Shattuck, Oklahoma. I could never understand why people leaving Russia had to leave through Germany. Odessa was a good port but anyone leaving Russia as immigrants had to go to Germany.

I recall my first shift in the fire room. I walked to the fire room and opened the door. A blast of heat hit me dead in the face. It reminded me of my time stoking the boilers on the Black Sea Fleet. I saw a stoker leaning on his shovel handle and when the cool air hit him, he turned and waved at me. He picked up his shove, handed it to me and disappeared out the door. His shift was over. I thought of Sergei and the friends I had made in the Black Sea Fleet. It took a while to get back in the swing of using a scoop shovel and the man in charge of the fire room was watching all of us. When someone began to slacken off, he barked orders. He made sure everyone was working. Helmut told me that several people had tried to pay for their passage to America by stoking the fireboxes on the boilers but very few were successful. There was one other man paying for his passage by working in the fire room but he was paying his whole fare that way and his shift was longer then mine.

My duty was moving coal from the bunkers to the section in front of the boiler. This meant I had to climb on the coal and scoop it out of the bunker into the holding pen in front of the boiler where another man placed the coal into the firebox of the boiler with a scoop shovel. We worked in shifts and we would be in the coal bunker then we would be feeding the firebox. Working in the fire room was dirty. Coal dust was everywhere and you had to be careful because dust can be explosive. The regular crew was used to the hard work but I was a shoemaker. I used my hands a lot but not for the heavy work of shoveling coal. I had a pair of work clothes, which consisted of a heavy pair of pants, long sleeve shirt and a cloth around my neck for wiping sweat and to keep sparks from going down my shirt. It was hot in the fire room but you had to wear the heavy clothes for protection from the heat and sparks. When my shift was finished, I washed out my work clothes along with the others on my shift and hung them up to dry. I always wore the same work clothes, saving my better clothes when I arrived in America. We did have an area to take a salt-water shower which was better than wearing the coal dust. I had grown soft by working in a shoe shop and when I was off my shift, I laid down on my bunk. I looked out the porthole and the stars were shining bright. I thought of arriving in America and drifted off to sleep. I woke up and I had slept through supper and was hungry but Helmut saved some food for me.

I asked one of the officers if I could go up on deck and he said I couldn't because that was for the First and Second Class Passengers and the crew members that worked that area of the ship. Steerage only could look out the portholes and walk the passageways in the lower part of the ship. That night, I looked out the porthole at the stars and they had never seemed so bright and everything seemed peaceful. I couldn't wait to arrive in America.

The trip became routine. I had a two-hour session stoking the boilers in the morning then another two-hour session in the afternoon. The rest of the time was my own. I became adjusted to the shovel and it was good to be working again. Several crew members stopped and told me I was one of the best working passengers they had ever had on the ship. My German was not good enough to carry on a good conversation so Helmut helped me and translated when I didn't know the correct word in German. The crew members told me stories of their life in Germany and I told them stories of Russia. They had made many trips to America and gave me some very good advice when I got off the ship, what to do and what not to do.

Staying in the cabin was dull when I was not on duty because I had always been an active person, I even looked forward to my session on the boilers and when I became really bored, I went to the boiler room to relive any crew member. I just had to have something to do.

Land was sighted and, my heart jumped and I almost cried. The day I had waited for years had arrived, we were approaching America. Helmut and I opened the porthole and didn't care if we were splashed or not. We craned our necks to look forward and could barely see a thin black line that was the coastline. That line grew thicker and thicker. I wanted to see the Statue of Liberty but I knew we were arriving at Boston, not New York City. The coastline grew closer and closer then I saw the buildings and two tugs came out and gently pushed the ship to the docks. I went to the hold while crew members on deck threw ropes to men waiting on the docks. A crane lifted an empty net and lowered it into the hold. I helped put the Boston crates into the net then they were lifted and disappeared out of the hold. Another net was lowered and we filled it. We repeated this until all the identified crates were removed. About one third of the passengers disembarked at Boston. We had one night in Boston while the ship was refueled and took on supplies. I didn't have enough money so Helmut and I stayed on the ship and looked at the lights out the porthole. The next morning, tugs pushed the ship away from the docks and we headed south. Helmut informed me the Statue of Liberty was at our next stop.

The trip to New York took most of the day and I was amazed how much larger New York was than Boston. I thought Odessa was large, but the buildings in New York were gigantic. I saw buildings that must have been 25 or 30 stories tall. Then I saw the Statue of Liberty and she was beautiful. She was standing with her arm raised personally welcoming me to America. Tears welled in my eyes and I was told to report to the hold. Most of the remaining cargo and passengers were unloaded at New York. I thought of the sweat shops Rabbi Blatt told me about and how I should go to Texas. I remember him telling me that New York had a quota on immigrants but Texas had no such quota. Just as in Boston, we unloaded passengers and their crates from the hold. We didn't spend the night in New York. Just as soon as the passengers and luggage were on shore, we left the docks and I watched the Statue of Liberty and then the buildings disappear and we headed for Texas.

I had no idea how far Texas was from New York. Since New York was just a couple of hours from Boston, I thought Texas was also a couple of hours away. I knew we would be docking in Galveston soon. Several hours passed and I asked Helmut how far Texas was. He told me we had to go down the east coast of the United States, across the Gulf of Mexico to Galveston. This was the first time I realized how large the United States was. It was almost as big as Russia. Instead of waiting for Galveston, we went back to working in the fire room. Helmut said it would be a couple of days before we reached Galveston.

I had been informed that I had to go through immigration, which included a health inspection. For the first time in my life I felt queasy in my stomach. What if I didn't pass the health inspection. I also heard they sent people back to Europe if they had an eye disease. We were given papers on the ship to fill out. I was filling my papers out in Russian and I noticed people were helping others that could not read or write. Then my heart sank. The papers said I had to have enough money to buy a train ticket to my final destination.

I had a total of 75 cents to my name. Helmut had borrowed a map from an officer on the ship and he pointed out that Dallas was 200 or 300 miles from Galveston. I knew I didn't have enough money for a train ticket. I told Helmut my problem and he said he had 50 cents he could loan me. I asked several people and I was told that the train ticket to Dallas cost $2.50. With the money from Helmut, I had $1.50. Helmut told me that several passengers had borrowed money from the crew members then returned it when they had gone through customs. I went to several crew members and very quickly had the $2.50 for my fare. One named Karl told me I was a good worker and that he was glad to loan me the money. Other crew members said if I needed more, they would gladly loan it. I suddenly realized we would be docking in Galveston soon and I would never see these friends ever again. I could feel the tears welling up and took all the energy I had not to cry. I wanted to be alone so I could cry and let my emotions go. The times in Bremerhaven and on the ship were not easy. They were not that difficult but I had met so many friends that I knew I would never see again.

We had passed down the east coast, rounded the Florida Keys then headed out into open water. Helmut told me we were taking the fastest route to Galveston, which was straight across the Gulf of Mexico instead of following the coast. I had my last shift in the fire room then was informed we were approaching Galveston. I went up, looked out the porthole and saw the coastline approaching. Galveston was not a large city like Boston or New York. Helmut told me there had been a hurricane several years before that had completely wiped out the city and it had not fully recovered. Being from Russia, I didn't understand what a hurricane was and how it could do so much damage.

The ship went by two islands and up a river to the docks and I had already taken my shower and was packed and ready to leave the ship. All the crew members came to say goodbye to me, even though they were getting off the ship. We had our own gangplank to leave the ship and I walked and held my head up high because I was entering the United States. We all were taken to the Galveston Island Immigration Station. There were people that spoke every language and men in uniform were directing people. Customs was very quick and insignificant. I was taken to a holding area with the steerage passengers. The First and Second Class passengers were taken to a different area and I could see they were given better treatment. I found later that very few of them had to go through the health inspection. My name was called and the only thing they checked were my eyes. He said I passed and stamped my papers. The only other stop I made was a counter to verify that I had enough money to get to my destination. I had my $2.50 wrapped in a handkerchief and proudly announced that I was going to Dallas and showed them the money. The man behind the counter said "OK" with a deadpan expression on his face and called for the next person in line. I knew he saw hundreds of people each week and must be a boring job. I saw Helmut and Karl and most of the guys from the fire room. They did not have to go through customs because they were leaving on the ship.

Everyone wished me luck and again repeated it was good to work with me. There were a few of the guys not there and I was told they were big guys but had soft hearts and did not like good byes. They all left except Helmut and Karl. I gave the money back and I asked where the Travelers Aid Society was located. They were not sure since they had never used their services but after looking around, we found the office. They were taking off for Galveston and we shook hands then hugged. I knew this was the last time we would meet in this life. I watched them walk away and I approached the office. I knew very little English and gave the man behind the counter a piece of paper with Solomon's name and address. I said, "Dallas, please."

The man realized I didn't speak English but he spoke German and asked if this is where I wanted to go. I told him this was my brother and showed him my passport and papers. He told me he would send a telegram to Solomon and if I needed to spend the night, they had rooms. After the telegram was sent he took me to a room and was given a hot meal and a cup of coffee. I took out my 75 cents and he grabbed my hand and told me "No," the meal and coffee are free. I knew America was going to be a great place. So many things were racing through my mind. The trip had been much easier than I had thought. I had imagined all types of problems arising but nothing materialized. I surveyed the area around the immigration office then walked outside and around the building. I saw the Kaiser Wilhelm sitting at the dock and I stood there in silence. A short but important chapter in my life was coming to a close.

It was early morning and I began walking along the docks and watched the activity. Ships were being loaded and unloaded and I was trying to adjust to the fact that I was in America. After an hour or two I returned to the Traveler's Aid Office and was informed that I had received a telegram from Solomon Kerbel. He had wired the money for a train ticket to Dallas and the ticket was waiting. I thanked the man behind the counter profusely then he escorted me to the train station, about six blocks away. He talked with the conductor and he told me that he told the conductor that I was going to Dallas but did not speak English. I said goodbye to the Traviler's Aid Office worker and thanked him for his help and knew everyone in America would be this friendly.

This is the immigration Building in Galveston.

The conductor escorted me to the train and to my seat and he put my bag in the overhead. I sat there for about 30 minutes when the whistle blew and the train began moving. The excitement I felt was beyond description. I was in America, on an American train going to see my brother. What could be better? Then there was a note of sadness. It could be better if the rest of the family was on the train with me.

Galveston was on an island and we crossed a bridge to the mainland. In a short time, the train pulled into Houston and came to a stop. The conductor walked by me and motioned for me to remain seated. I'm sure he did this so I did not get off the train. I knew I was in good hands. People got on the train and everyone nodded and smiled and spoke but I didn't understand what they were saying. I nodded and smiled back. The train pulled out and the countryside was flat just as in Germany around the North Sea. We passed farms and herds of cattle and horses and I was amazed at the expanse of the country. There was an openness here that Europe did not have. The next town we came to was Conroe. The train stopped again and as before the conductor motioned for me to remain seated. Each time the train stopped I waited for the conductor to come by and each time he motioned for me to remain seated.

I began to think that Texas was as big as Russia except this train stopped at every small town. In Russia the trains only stopped at the larger towns and cities. I watched people get on or get off and everyone was courteous and friendly. The train was pulling out of a town by the name of Waxahachie and the conductor stopped at my seat. He told me Dallas was the next stop but of course I didn't understand what he said but I had an idea. Sure enough as the train began slowing down, the conductor shook his head yes and I knew this was Dallas. I remained seated until the other passengers left the train. My stomach was queasy. I had not seen Solomon in several years and what was I going to say to him. If he wasn't at the station, what was I to do?

All my fears were in vain. I walked to the door and there was Solomon on the platform. He waved at me and he greeted me in Russian. It was good to hear words I understood. I returned his greeting and jumped from the train and Solomon ran towards me. When we met, he extended his hand but I pushed it aside and hugged him. He said, "Welcome to America." We had a reunion that only brothers can have. He asked me about home and how things were and I told him briefly about the pogroms and he had heard of them and was devastated but he assured me that nothing like that would ever happen in America. I then told him about being in the Russian Army and getting a passport and going to Germany and then on to America. Solomon then told me how wonderful America was and he hoped to bring the whole family over.

Chapter Ten

The Justin Boot Company and Tandy Leather

Our first conversation was about Mama and the rest of the family. Solomon wanted to know every detail about the family and Odessa. I told him that I thought Mama had been writing him letters and he said he was receiving all of her letters but he wanted to know what was really going on. I told him that Rosa and Gueti were well and Papa was the same. Papa never changed from one year to another. I talked about Odessa, the people and the shops. Papa's shoe shop was doing very well until the pogrom. Odessa was trying to heal itself but wounds and hatreds so severe

This is a photograph of Solomon and me taken in Dallas just after I arrived. We sent a copy to Mama and Papa. I am the one seated.

caused by the riot were very slow to heal. I also told him that the stage was set for revolution in Russia and I didn't know what was going to happen.

We talked as people rushed by us, then we walked out of the train station. The first thing I noticed was how drab the train station was, not like the very ornate stations in Europe. I mentioned this to Solomon and he told me that Texas was a new country and buildings were built to be used, not for beauty. The street was amazing. I had never seen so many automobiles anywhere and among the automobiles were the streetcars. Among all this activity there were horse-drawn wagons. Here was the old with the new. America was indeed going to be a wonderful place. Solomon had a taxi waiting for us and I had never driven in an automobile before. The taxi driver was very courteous, put my one satchel in the car and off we went. The automobile was amazing.

I asked how this thing was powered and taxi driver explained the gasoline engine and the power train, but I didn't understand anything he said. The first place we stopped was Uncle Herman's Butcher Shop. He was Mama's brother and had changed his name from Shmukler to Golden. He had been in America seven or eight years and had sponsored Solomon when he came to America. Even though he had been in this country only a few years he had a thriving butcher shop, Golden's Butcher Shop. He opened this shop because he had one in Russia. I hadn't seen Uncle Herman since he left Russia and was surprised at how successful he was. He worked hard in his shop and built up a good business and was known for the best meat in Dallas. He proudly told me that not all of his customers were Jewish. He said a lot of Christians came to his shop because they knew the meat was fresh and clean.

One story he enjoyed telling was about his famous pickles. There were several families that had known uncle Herman in Russia. One man told Uncle Herman that he should make the pickles as he did in his in Rovno. So he began making his pickles and had them in two large wooden barrels in the back of the shop. A Christian lady bought some and told him they were wonderful and when she came to the shop she always asked for his "Kosher Pickles" and the name stuck. His pickles became famous and one day a man came to his shop and bought some and said they were very good. That man was from a company named Swift. That company purchased his method of making the "Kosher Dill" and began marketing them. The Kosher Dill was famous and Uncle Herman started them.

Aunt Rachel, Herman's wife was there and we had a good reunion. As customers came into the shop, Uncle Herman introduced me to them and I can't remember how many came to the shop. Between the customers, we talked about Russia. He had to move also when the Czar gave our land to the Grand Duke Ernst Ludwig in Germany and Uncle Herman halted the conversation. He said it was not good to talk of the bad times. We began talking of the happier times in Russia when Solomon and I were boys and life was simpler. I recalled how simple life was in Roshen and how complicated it became in Odessa. Uncle Herman then asked about the pogrom in Odessa. This was a topic I did not want to discuss. He said he had heard of what had happened. I talked a little then he asked about the Self Defense in Odessa. I asked how he knew about that. He said something like the Self Defense cannot be kept quiet and said that he knew I helped organize the Self Defense. I couldn't understand how he knew, then he told me that Mama had written and told him. I explained that it was a topic I did not enjoy talking about and we went back to the happier subjects. We spent several hours with Uncle Herman and Aunt Rachel. The taxi driver stayed in the shop with us and we took off again. All too soon my first ride came to an end at Solomon's apartment just off Commerce Street in downtown Dallas.

The apartment was just two blocks from where Solomon worked as an accountant for the Railway Commission. I was impressed with his title and the job he held and I was amazed that he had the job. In Russia, you always took over the job from your father as it had always been. Solomon explained that anyone could get a job in America at anything they wanted to do. This confirmed my thoughts that America was going to be a great place. The first person I met was Solomon's landlady, Mrs. Tecza, and she had a supper prepared when I arrived. She and her husband were Jews and had emigrated from Poland in 1894. They had planned to make a new life in America but he was killed in a train accident. He worked for the railroad and a boiler exploded two years ago. They had no children and she was alone and very glad to have Solomon as a tenant.

She spoke Polish and English along with a little German and Russian. I knew a few words in Polish and between our languages, we had a good conversation. She told Solomon that the first thing I must learn is English and Solomon told her he would help me. Solomon had been telling his neighbors for weeks that I was coming and everyone came to introduce themselves and I couldn't believe how friendly everyone was. The neighbors had come from all over Europe and from different states in the United States and everyone was friendly.

The evening wore on and I was getting tired. I knew Solomon had taken off work to meet me and this had been a tiring day. His boss had given him several days off to get me settled. I unpacked my satchel and took out the most precious possession, the oil lamp that Mama had given me. I took out my leather tools and carefully cleaned them. This was from habit because they had not been used but Papa made sure we cleaned our tools every day. We turned in early for a long day tomorrow. I don't think I slept a wink that first night in America. I was too excited. I wanted to get a job and bring the whole family to America.

The sun rose early. This was my first sunrise in America but had a little sad feeling about the family and not seeing the sunrise in Russia again. Your first home is always special and Roshen always had a special place in my memory even though the town didn't exist any more. The first thing Solomon did was take me to a shop where I could buy some new clothes. I only had one shirt and pair of pants. All the other clothes had been worn out shoveling coal on the ship. I was proud of my new clothes. I looked like an American.

This was Wednesday and we spent this day sightseeing around Dallas in a taxi. I was surprised how large and open Dallas was. The houses had so much land around them, not like in Russia or Germany where the houses are built next to each other and are so small. I surely thought royalty must live in some of the houses we saw. They were enormous with large spacious formal gardens. Solomon told me just ordinary people lived in these houses and they worked hard and made a good living. I could see nothing ordinary about these houses. Only the Czar and his family would live in these houses in Russia.

We drove by many fine houses then had lunch at a little delicatessen run by a little Jewish lady from Germany. First thing she told me was she bought all of her meat from Uncle Herman. After lunch we sat and talked and I told Solomon that I wanted to bring the whole family to America. Solomon asked if Mama and Papa would come to America. He said their roots ran deep in Russia and thought they would never leave. I knew he was right. They would not leave Russia. I left because the pogrom in Odessa had mortally wounded my roots and I had no trouble leaving. I thought back on the pogrom. Smuggling in the weapons and ammunition, then seeing the riot at the Synagogue, then the burning building and the dead. But the one overpowering image was that little girl. That one innocent life snuffed out did more to kill any roots I had in Russia. The image of that little girl demanded that I be nonviolent. I saw what people can do to each other and promised myself that I would never become one of them.

The next day was Thursday and Solomon went back to work. We had stopped by Uncle Herman's and I told him that I wanted to repair Solomon's shoes but needed a few pieces of leather and asked where to get them. I don't know where he got the leather but he brought leather and several shoes from his house and I began repairing shoes.

Friday, Solomon was preparing for the Sabbath. On my tour of Dallas, we drove by many fine churches and the Synagogue. I had fallen away from my faith and told Solomon I would not go the Synagogue with him. He stared at me but didn't ask why. I told him I had seen too much hate and anger and was afraid attending would bring back these nightmares.

For two weeks, I repaired shoes for Solomon, Uncle Herman and Aunt Rachel, Mrs. Tecza and neighbors of Solomon. For her kindness I made a new pair of shoes for Mrs. Tecza. Uncle Herman provided all the leather and I stayed busy. During all this I was learning English from Solomon and Mrs. Tecza. Solomon had come in from work. We had eaten and were settling in for the evening when there was a knock on the door. Solomon had a subscription to the Dallas newspaper and noticed an advertisement from the Justin Boot Company. They were advertising for a person to help make boots and shoes in a shop they had just opened in Fort Worth, even though the main office was in Nocona, Texas. He showed the paper and I wanted the job.

The next day Uncle Herman came by the apartment with an expectant look on his face. He quickly came in and told me he had found me a job in Nocona, Texas, and they had a store in Fort Worth, which was about 30 miles west of Dallas. He said that one of his best customers was Herman Justin who owned the boot company in Nocona. Even though he lived in Nocona, he came to Dallas to buy his meat and especially the Kosher Pickles from Uncle Herman.

Uncle Herman said proudly, "Herman Justin says no one makes a pickle like Herman Golden." He told Mr. Justin that I had just arrived from Russia and was an experienced boot maker. Mr. Justin said his business was expanding and he needed another good boot maker and wanted to talk to me. Uncle Herman produced a piece of paper with the address on Jennings Street in Fort Worth of the Justin Boot Company. Mr. Justin said I was to be there tomorrow to meet with him. If Uncle Herman was this excited about the prospect, it must be a good job. I didn't tell Uncle Herman that I had seen the advertisement in the newspaper for the job at the Justin Boot Company. When Solomon came home I told him what had happened and that I was not going to mention the newspaper advertisement. Solomon agreed, it was best to let Uncle Herman handle this.

Solomon gave enough money for a round trip on the Interurban, which ran between Dallas and Fort Worth. I was nervous. Mr. Justin seemed to be a very nice man but a tough businessman. I spoke no English and a little German and Mr. Justin only spoke English. The first problem was to find Jennings Street in Fort Worth. I was terrified I would get lost and wander around Fort Worth for hours. Solomon told me to give the address to the conductor on the Interurban and everything would be fine. There was a station on the Interurban not far from Solomon's apartment. When I arrived, there were about 30 people waiting. I felt so proud to be in America with a group of Americans on my own for the first time.

The car stopped and I held back while everyone got on. One elderly lady was preparing to climb on the car and I helped her up. She turned and thanked me very much and I felt ten feet tall at that moment. I gave the piece of paper to the conductor and then held out my hand with the money. He read the address then took the money for the fare. I don't know how much the fare was. The lady I helped on the car walked up and asked if I needed help.

I didn't know what to say and all I knew to say was "Fort Worth." She said she was also going to Fort Worth and would help me. She took the paper from the conductor and told him I was a nice young man as she patted my hand and said she would make sure I would get to where I was going. Of course I didn't understand much of what was said but from her facial expression and the way she patted my hand I knew I could trust her. America certainly was a great country.

The trip to Fort Worth took almost two hours because we had to make numerous stops in Dallas and had to change cars at the main station. As the car rolled on the tracks, it made a grinding sound now and then and I could hear the electricity on the arm that was attached to the overhead wires and I thought of the overhead wires in Odessa and how they were used. The lady took me by the hand and we got off the car and onto the one heading west to Fort Worth. The countryside outside of Dallas was beautiful. Farms and ranches spread out on both sides of the tracks. We stopped at Arlington to let some people off and other people got on. More farms and ranches spread out and then we were approaching Fort Worth and I saw fewer farms and more houses. The car was on the main street in Fort Worth, which was brick, and it slowly rocked back and forth. We passed the City Hall and I was amazed. It was made of red stone and was a beautiful building. The station was just a few blocks from the City Hall. The lady took my arm and we got off the car and headed down the street. She was looking at the paper and I wanted to tell her that if she could direct me, I could find the boot company but I didn't speak English and she spoke no Russian. The boot company was about six blocks from the station and she walked the whole six blocks, went into the building with me and announced that I was there. I thanked her again and again and wanted to pay her but she patted my hand again and said, "You are welcome."

John Justin came out, thanked the lady and told me they were expecting me. She waved and walked out the door. Through this whole thing I never got the lady's name or where she was going. I wanted to thank her properly. John motioned toward a chair and I sat down. He disappeared and returned with his father, Herman. I stood up, we shook hands and I greeted him in Russian and he seemed to be impressed. Another man came up and introduced himself in Russian. His name was Boris Egnatovich. He told me that Mr. Golden said I spoke Russian. Boris then explained that he too had been a boot maker in Russia and had come to the United States and had been working for Mr. Justin for almost two years. I told him that I had made boots in Russia and in Bremerhaven before coming to America.

Boris was our interpreter. Mr. Justin and I talked for about an hour and a half. He told me how he had left Lafayette, Indiana, and moved to Texas. We discussed the different types of leather used to make boots and shoes and why certain leather was better for boots and other leather for shoes. I showed him tools and he inspected them. He then brought out a boot for me to inspect. I wasn't familiar with the style of American boots because they were not made in Russia, but I knew the stitching.

We discussed the different types of heels on the American boot and shoe. After our conversation, Mr. Justin slapped me on the back and told me that I knew my boots and shoes. He also said that he could talk with a man for 30 seconds and could tell if he had a good knowledge of shoe making. Boris told me I had been hired and could start this minute if I wanted. I didn't know what to say. I shook his hand then gave him a good Russian hug and he gave me a good hug. We then talked about the village of Roshen and growing up in my father's shoe shop and moving to Odessa. Mr. Justin was very observant and noticed the change in my voice. Boris immediately began talking to Mr. Justin. His face saddened and a look of sympathy came over him.

I knew Boris was telling him about the pogrom. Mr. Justin was also very wise because he never mentioned or asked about it. He then quickly changed the conversation to his childhood in Indiana and moving to Texas where he began repairing boots and establishing the boot company. I was taken to the back where there were several workers and introduced to all of them. I couldn't believe Mr. Justin had this many people working for him. In Russia the government would own the company.

That day passed very quickly. The first thing I did was take out my tools and inspect them. Mr. Justin walked up and told me that now he knew I was an excellent boot maker. He said he could tell a good boot maker by the way he takes care of his tools. Mr. Justin was a lot like Papa but Papa was a lot taller. Mr. Justin was only about five feet six inches tall and papa was almost six feet four inches tall. Boris spent the entire day with me. He had a pad of paper and he wrote the English words that he thought I should know. He wrote the name of each tool in Russian, then the English word beside it. Boris and I became very good friends. The day ended at 6:00 p.m. and Mr. Justin came and congratulated me again. To my surprise he paid me for the first day. He said he remembered when he was first getting started and how precious money was in the first few weeks. He said he would pay me each day until I got on my feet, then I would be paid once a week.

Boris walked out the front door with me and escorted me to the Interurban Station. As I was getting on, he handed me another piece of paper. On this piece of paper had written the exact instructions to the boot company. He said that if I got lost, give the paper to someone and they would direct me to the factory. I told Boris that America was a God-blessed country, if you could walk up to a stranger and have them direct you to your destination. He agreed, turned and left.

Solomon, Uncle Herman, Aunt Rachel and Mrs. Tecza

were all waiting as I entered the apartment. I had so much to tell them and didn't know where to begin. Mrs. Tecza had prepared a supper for all of us and we had a celebration. I spent the next three hours telling them all about the Justin Boot Company and how friendly everyone was. I explained how this elderly lady on the Interurban took me by the hand and walked with me to the factory and how I wanted to thank her but didn't even get her name. Aunt Rachel said that people are friendly like that here.

Everyone left and I was still excited and told Solomon that I had to learn better English. He told me it would be easy and the best way was to immerse myself in the language. He told me to listen to the people and I would be able to pick up words then sentences. He said that before I knew it I would be speaking like a native. The hour was late but I was much too excited to sleep. Solomon went over the words Boris had written and he helped me pronounce each one in English.

After I went to bed, I lay there thinking of the threshold on which I was standing. I wondered how a poor Russian immigrant could be in Dallas, Texas, and working at the Justin Boot Company in Fort Worth. The loneliness I had felt for Mama, Papa, Rosa and Gueti was not as strong.

Chapter Eleven
A Jew in America

My salary at the Justin Boot Company was $4.50 a week. I never knew one man could make so much money. Solomon was only making $4.00 a week. I knew America was going to be a great country but I didn't know how great. I paid the rent for two weeks because I felt I owed it to Solomon. He had been buying clothes, food and I was living under his roof. The trip from Dallas to Fort Worth was different each day. There were certain people that made the trip with me and we always greeted each other but there were always new faces and they were friendly. On the trip I studied the farms and ranches as we passed and told myself that someday I was going to own my own farm. I was going to be an American farmer.

My English was improving every day. I set a goal to learn a new word each day and Boris helped me. My first real conversation in English was with a man named Dave Tandy, who delivered leather once a week to the factory or when it was needed. I needed a new leather knife. Boris told me that Mr. Tandy had the knives and I could get one from him. I told Mr. Justin that I needed a new knife because the one Papa had given me was getting old and the blade was getting very thin. I was putting a pair of heels on a boot when Boris came to me and said I was to go to the back door where deliveries were made. There was Mr. Tandy talking to Mr. Justin. I was introduced to Mr. Tandy as the leather man. I had seen him when he was delivering the leather and had even spoken to him once or twice. I said in English, "I want to purchase a new leather knife."

There were other places to which he delivered leather and always carried tools for sale. I said to Boris in Russian that I didn't have the money at this time and Boris told me to tell Mr. Tandy in English. I said, "I do not have money now, but will pay later." Mr. Justin paid for the knife, which cost 25 cents, and told me he would take it out of my salary. Mr. Tandy handed the knife to me. This surprised me. Where else in the world would your employer pay for something that you wanted because you didn't have the money. This was the first knife I actually owned because Papa had given all the other tools to me. I held the knife in my hand and turned it around and around. I thanked Mr. Justin and Mr. Tandy and returned to my workbench and began sharpening the knife. I finished putting the heels on the boots, which took twice as much time because I was admiring my knife and thinking of the unlimited possibilities that were open to me.

Each day as I waited for the Interurban in Dallas, I kept looking for the lady that helped me the first day, but I never saw her again. I don't know who she was, where she came from or whatever happened to her. When I learned better English, I asked several people if they knew her but no one remembered her. I finally decided that God had sent her to guide my footsteps that day.

I had been living in the apartment with Solomon for about three months and he came in late one evening. He said he had gone out and that wasn't unusual. Then he began coming in late several evening each week and that was unusual. One morning he said there was someone he wanted me to meet. He had a girlfriend. He tried to bring her to the apartment but she refused. A single girl did not go to a man's apartment. The following Sunday we were to have lunch together. The week went by very slowly. I was anxious to meet this girl. Solomon told me her name was Sally Johnson and her family had moved to Texas from Tennessee in 1840 when it was still a republic. I didn't know Texas history at this time and these stories of the Texas Republic and other states meant nothing to me. We had a very nice lunch and Solomon acted differently around her and I knew he was serious. After the lunch, I asked Solomon if Sally was a Jew. He said no but they had discussed this and her family had no problem with this. My confidence in America was confirmed. In Russia a girl like Sally would have never been allowed to court a Jew. This was the time I thought about moving to Fort Worth. I brought up the subject to Solomon and it caught him off guard. He didn't understand why I wanted to move. I explained that he was seeing someone that he was serious about and I felt I was in the way and that the trip to Fort Worth and back each day was long and boring. It really wasn't, but I told him that. I said I was determined to move to Fort Worth and he accepted the fact.

Mr. Justin had become like a father to me. He showed emotions that Papa had never shown and this was new to me. I informed him that I wanted to find a place in Fort Worth and he told me he would help me find an apartment. Tuesday morning Mr. Justin told me to come with him. We were leaving the factory. We walked out front and his new automobile was parked there, a new Packard. I had never seen such a fine automobile. I had only been in one other automobile and that was the taxi Solomon hired when I first arrived. We drove to Berry Street to an apartment house and I was introduced to Mr. Anderson, the landlord. He looked me up and down and said, "I have known Mr. Justin for several years and if he recommends you, you are OK."

He then said, "You are a Jew, aren't you?" I said that I was, not knowing what else to say and not knowing what was going to happen. He then said, "That is fine, as long as you pay the rent." I was taken to an apartment with three rooms, kitchen, bedroom and living room and it was furnished. Mr. Anderson said the rent was $10.00 a month. My salary at the boot factory was now $5.50 a week and I said this was a very fine apartment. To my surprise, Mr. Justin paid the first month's rent and told me he would take it out of my salary as he had done with the knife. Mr. Anderson handed me the key to the door and Mr. Tandy said we should get back to the shop. I stood in the middle of the living room amazed that I was in my own apartment in America. I had been in Texas just over four months and already I had a good job and a place of my own. It was difficult for me to comprehend that I had gone from an immigrant from Russia to a worker in America.

Solomon and Uncle Herman came to Fort Worth with me to get settled on Saturday. This was the Sabbath and I felt uncomfortable but Uncle Herman told me that it was OK and we had to adjust to America and work when it was necessary. He also told me he wanted to know where I was going to be living. I packed the clothes I had in a few boxes and we rode the Interurban to my new apartment. The station in Fort Worth was just a few blocks from my apartment and also just a few blocks from the boot factory. This was going to be much more convenient than getting up each morning to ride from Dallas. Uncle Herman approved of the apartment and he and Solomon left. I spent the rest of the day unpacking my clothes and meeting the neighbors in the other apartments.

Boris took me to my first rodeo held at the Fort Worth arena. It was exciting to watch the cowboys ride the broncs and the bulls and the roping events. It was just as exciting to watch the crowd. I even bought my first cowboy hat at the rodeo and Boris helped me pick it out. It was a felt hat and fit low on my forehead. I felt like a cowboy even if I didn't talk like one. All I needed now was a girlfriend. Solomon had Sally and I wanted a girlfriend. Boris had a girlfriend whose name was Ellen and he asked if I would like to go for a drive on the next Sunday. Of course I said yes. He told me her parents were going along because a girl didn't go out unescorted. He also told me that Ellen had two sisters but they would not be going with us. Still I would meet the parents and perhaps I could meet the sisters later on. I had fallen away from my faith. I was looking forward to the Sunday Drive but thought perhaps I should attend Temple.

I had met many Jews in Fort Worth and had even seen the Synagogue. Many people invited me to attend with them but I didn't and did not explain. I couldn't bring myself to attend. I was terrified all the memories would come flooding back that I had suppressed and the nightmares would return. I did prepare food for the Sabbath even though I didn't go to the Temple.

I had an icebox in my apartment and twice a week the iceman brought ice. I never locked my apartment, I put my card for how many pounds of ice I needed and like magic the block of ice appeared. As I said, I never locked my apartment and was never once troubled by an intruder. We didn't lock doors in Fort Worth, we didn't have too. I thought of Papa and how he told me I would not be able to observe the dietary laws when I left Odessa and I knew how right he was. I hadn't followed the law for several years but was doing better being around Solomon. I had even fallen from praying to God but I said a prayer this time even though I was no longer a religious man. I knew I was blaming God for what happened in Odessa but then this same God brought me to America and I thanked Him in my prayer.

I left my apartment and walked to the Synagogue. Solomon had his yarmulke but I no longer had one, but knew one would be provided. I entered the door and a warm feeling came over me. It was good to be here. I saw familiar faces I had met in Fort Worth and one man told me he was wondering how long before I came. The Rabbi's name was Axelrod and he introduced me to many people after the service. Some I had seen before and some were new faces. The Temple was Orthodox and I knew I couldn't speak to the women at the Temple but I saw a young girl. Her face was young and beautiful and her eyes shone. I was introduced before the congregation and was even invited to hold the Torah when the altar was opened. After the service I met more members and saw the young girl again.

Her name was Rebekah. I didn't speak to her but I knew I would see her again. Several men had heard I was in Fort Worth because Uncle Herman made sure my presence was known. I returned to my apartment with the face of Rebekah in my mind and I knew I would see her again. I normally didn't prepare food for the Sabbath because I had not been obeying the laws but this time I was prepared. I did no work this Sabbath and when it ended I took a walk around Fort Worth and stopped at a local restaurant and had a meal. This wasn't done by most Jews because of the dietary law. I didn't go out to eat often, not because of the law but because I couldn't afford it, but I did tonight.

The sun rose Sunday morning and I felt much better, having been to Temple. At 12:30 in the afternoon, there was a knock on the door. Boris was standing there. He was Christian and attended the Lutheran Church regularly. Boris was dressed in a suit and tie and my heart sank. I didn't have such fine clothes to wear. I had a clean shirt and pants on but no suit. He assured me it would be all right. We walked out to the street and he was driving Mr. Justin's new Packard. I knew he was one of his best employees but to drive his new car was beyond my comprehension. We drove to White Settlement Drive to the house where Ellen lived. It was a very nice house, one story with six rooms. Boris knocked on the door and Mr. Jorgensen, Ellen's father ,invited us in. He also was dressed in a suit and I felt completely out of place and wished I had not come. Boris told him I had just come to America from Russia. Mr. Jorgensen told me he remembered when he came from Germany and understood the problems of getting settled. This was his way of letting me know he understood the way I was dressed but I still felt uncomfortable.

Mrs. Jorgensen and Ellen entered the room attired in their automobile clothes, large hats that were tied down with scarves and goggles. Boris said he was driving a Packard that was enclosed and the scarves and goggles were left behind. Of course the hats were worn because respectable women did not go out without a hat. We had a very pleasant afternoon. We drove through Fort Worth and stopped and had an ice cream. Boris was acting like Solomon with his girlfriend and I thought that perhaps both would be married soon.

Mrs. Jorgensen mentioned her other two daughters but Mr. Jorgensen changed the subject very quickly. We talked about the weather, Mr. Justin's Packard, and even the brick streets in Fort Worth. Ellen mentioned her sisters and her father changed the subject again. Mr. Jorgensen mentioned that today was Sunday and a good day for church and this was telling me that a Jew was not acceptable for either of his daughters. I knew at this point Boris had told them I was a Jew and I was accepted as his friend but not acceptable for his daughters. I sat in silence during the return drive to their home and they were very cordial in their farewell and I knew it would be a final farewell. Ellen took my hand and said she truly enjoyed the afternoon and seemed to understand the situation I was in. Boris spoke very little during the drive to my apartment. I don't think he knew what to say. He did mention that he told Mr. Jorgensen that I was a Jew and a good worker and a good friend. He did this because they would have known I was a Jew. I wished I had never gone for the ride. A tinge of the anti-Jewish feeling came back. Boris assured me they had nothing against me but I knew I would never be acceptable for his daughters. I decided Jews should marry Jews and Christians should marry Christians.

Mr. Justin knew something was wrong Monday morning. I was eating lunch at my workbench when he came to me and began talking. This was unusual. Mr. Justin didn't normally talk to his employees at their workbench. He asked what was wrong. I avoided the subject and told him nothing. He said he knew when something was wrong with one of his employees and I had a problem. I knew it was useless to avoid the subject so I told him everything that happened yesterday. He sat down and said that even though this was America there were still problems. He continued and told me to reflect on the old country and compare it with America. He said people were killed in Europe for being a Jew. In America they don't let you see their daughters. It made me feel better and Boris apologized for what happened. He said he had no idea how Mr. Jorgensen felt about Jews but he should not have been told I was a Jew. I told Boris to look at me. I look like a Jew. He said Mr. Jorgensen was also an immigrant and had been in America about ten years and the people of Fort Worth didn't seem to have a problem with the Jews. I said they don't have a problem with us, they just don't want us to see their daughters. Boris had been very friendly to me until the daughters came into the conversation.

I turned all of my energy into making good boots and Mr. Justin complimented me on my work for the week. The Sabbath was approaching and I wanted to get back into my faith. I thought that maybe God had sent Mr. Jorgensen to get me back onto the right path and I was able to put any anger aside. I prepared food and left the apartment for the Temple. Again I was greeted by Rabbi Axelrod and other members. I saw Rebekah walking with her family down the sidewalk. Her father was Jacob Golitsyn, whom I had met the week before. I excused myself and went to greet Jacob. He introduced me to his wife Sarah, his son Aaron and his daughter Rebekah. I said it was a pleasure to meet such a fine family.

After the service, Mr. Golitsyn invited me to go for a ride in the park with them. He had a carriage and two horses. Aaron was invited to stay at the house and I took his place beside Mrs. Golitsyn, and Mr. Golitsyn sat next to Rebekah. The carriage had two seats, which faced and I sat across from Rebekah, but not allowed to sit next to her. Driving a carriage was work and Mr. Johnson, a Christian and a friend of Mr. Golitsyn, drove the carriage. He said he had come from Moscow six years ago and was very pleased to meet another Russian Jew. We drove through the park and saw people playing badminton and croquet and life seemed so serene. This was a radical change from my past. At this moment Mr. Golitsyn made the comment that life in Texas was very different from Russia and I immediately agreed.

We drove to their home, which was a very nice house, not far from my apartment. I was invited into their home and Mrs. Golitsyn and Rebekah excused themselves and I sat in the parlor with Jacob. As we walked through the door, he asked me to call him Jacob and I knew this was a very great honor. We talked for a few moments then he said that he wanted to hear about the Self Defense. I looked at him very fast and he told me that Herman Golden had said that I was in the Self Defense and he was proud of me and wanted everyone to know what I had done. Again, this was not a subject I wanted to discuss but knew there was no way around it. I explained how the Self Defense was formed, how I smuggled the guns and ammunition and practiced in the caves near Odessa and then about the pogroms. When I mentioned the pogrom, he said that perhaps we should change the subject. He told me he could tell by the change in my voice and my face it was not a pleasant subject. I nodded, said my farewell, and walked to my apartment.

Rebekah was a beautiful young girl and I thought for sure her father liked me. He had to, he asked me to call him by his first name. I had never felt this way about anyone and didn't know what to do. I felt confused. I was at my workbench and Mr. Justin came by and began talking again. This began to worry me. This was two times he came by my workbench. He asked if I had the same problem. I asked what problem? He then said that something was still wrong. I informed him of the ride Saturday and he chuckled. He then asked which was worse, my feelings about Mr. Jorgensen or Rebekah. This caught me off guard and I didn't answer him.

A letter came from Solomon and he had come by my apartment but I was not at home. I answered his letter and explained that I had gone for a ride with a family from the Temple. I attended Temple again, to see Rebekah more than to restore my faith. Sunday, I took the Interurban to Dallas and went to see Solomon. I told him all about Rebekah and that we had known each other for only two weeks. Solomon told me that in Russia this would never have been allowed because of the Matchmaker, but I don't think America had Matchmakers, at least not in Texas. I talked about my experience with the Jorgensen's and Solomon said that was to be expected. He said everyone had a prejudice against an individual or a group. I had a lot to learn about America. In Russia, prejudice meant violence but in America it was tolerated with peace, or usually was.

I became active in the Temple, but as I said more for Rebekah than my faith. Then Nathan moved to Fort Worth. He was a German Jew and was new to America. He attended Temple and I welcomed him along with everyone else. He had been a banker in Germany and had a job at a bank in Fort Worth. He spotted Rebekah the first Sabbath and I felt my first tinge of jealousy. What was worse, Rebekah spotted him. Mr. Golitsyn also thought that a banker would be better for his daughter than a boot maker. I saw less and less of Rebekah then her father old me they were getting married. This was three weeks after they met. I wished them all the happiness in the world and Rebekah took my hand and said that she hoped I understood. She said they had fallen in love when they first met but she didn't want to hurt me. Solomon attended the wedding with me and it was a good wedding. We had a good meal then returned to my apartment and I thought my world was falling apart.

God works in mysterious ways because the following

Tuesday, Mr. Jackson from Ardmore, Oklahoma, came to the shop. I was introduced to him and he said he and Herman were very good friends and he always enjoyed coming to Fort Worth. He had a shoe shop in Ardmore repairing boots and shoes and selling Mr. Justin's Boots. Mr. Justin told Mr. Jackson that I was one of his best workers. They left and in twenty or thirty minutes, Mr. Jackson returned. He told me he had been talking to Herman and wanted me to come to Ardmore and work for him. I asked what Mr. Justin thought about him trying to hire me away. He said it was up to me. My salary working for Mr. Justin was now up to $8.50 a week and Mr. Jackson offered $9.00 a week if I came to Ardmore. This was 50 cents a week more, which was a lot of money. He said that Ardmore was growing and he needed someone in the shop to help him. He explained that Ardmore was in the old Chickasaw Indian Nation and a lot of his customers were Indian, but they were civilized.

He then told me there was a sizeable Jewish population in the town. He also said cotton farming had been the main industry but said that cotton wears out the land and the oil industry was on the rise in the area. He said between the farmers, ranchers and oil field workers, he needed help in his shop. He explained that most of his customers were ranchers and the oil field workers that needed a good work boot. I told him that I had made boots for sailors in the Black Sea Fleet in Odessa, Russia, and could make a good boot. He said I was the worker he was looking for and told me to think about it. He left his name and address and left the factory with the boots he had purchased. I had never thought much about the Indians and wondered what they would be like. If the Indians around Ardmore were civilized, what were the other Indians going to be like?

Mr. Justin took me to lunch, which was not normal. He knew about the problems I had with Mr. Jorgensen and Rebekah and said that I should take Mr. Jackson up on his offer. He said he had known the man for several years and would trust him with his life. I said I had no problem with Mr. Jorgensen because I faced much more in Russia, but Rebekah was a little more difficult. He then told me I should take the job in Ardmore and if it didn't work out I could always return because I would always have a job at his factory. I told Mr. Justin that he had become like a father to me and I couldn't explain what working at the factory meant to me. He told me that I should get away for a while and that is when I took the job in Ardmore. Word spread that I was leaving the factory and everyone came to say goodbye. Boris came to my workbench and we shook hands. We were still friends but not as close as we had been before Mr. Jorgensen.

I wrote Mr. Jackson that night and told him I would take the job. The next week a telegram arrived from the Jackson Shoe Shop in Ardmore, Oklahoma. It said that I should pack everything and he would pay my expenses to Ardmore and a train ticket would be waiting for me at the MK&T depot. I took the telegram to Mr. Justin and he asked what I was waiting for? I then sent a telegram to Solomon that I was moving to Ardmore but it was not that far away. I went home and packed everything, especially Mama's oil lamp, very carefully. This oil lamp was the only connection I had with Russia. Mr. Anderson and his wife told me that I had been a very good tenant and were sad to see me leave, but glad that I was moving up.

The next morning, Solomon was at my door to accompany me to the station. I took my two satchels and my small box, which contained my prized lamp and headed toward the train station. Mr. Anderson came with us and at the station were Boris, Mr. Justin, and several of the other workers. I introduced Solomon to everyone and we talked for a while in the waiting room, then I heard the announcement the train was leaving for Oklahoma City. This was my train. Mr. Anderson shook my hand, thanked me for being such a good friend and stepped back. Boris grabbed my hand and wished me luck. I shook hands with the other people from the factory then Mr. Justin. He told me again I was a good worker and expected great things from me. Solomon grabbed me and hugged me and he agreed Ardmore was not that far. I heard the conductor announce "All Aboard," and I climbed onto the train. I took a seat and looked out the window at Solomon and my friends. I felt a twinge of sadness of leaving, then the whistle blew and the train moved and all the cars bumped and groaned against each other. The cars moved slowly then the pace quickened and the depot and my friends began to recede as the train headed out. I saw the tower from the city hall and the buildings began to pass. Fort Worth disappeared and farmland stretched out in front of me. I was off on a new adventure, to a place I had never been before. This seemed to be my lot in life, new adventures. I had been working for Mr. Justin almost one year and I thought that this is 1913 and two years ago I was still in Russia.

Ardmore was about 30 miles north of the Red River, which was the state line between Texas and Oklahoma, and about 100 miles north of Fort Worth. The trip took about four hours because the train stopped in every small town to take on water and let passengers on and off. I didn't know what to expect in Ardmore. Fort Worth was a big city and if Ardmore had a shoe shop, it must be a good size town or small city, even though I had never heard of it before. After passing through Denton, Gainesville in Texas and Thackerville and Marietta in Oklahoma, we arrived at Ardmore and Mr. Jackson was at the train station. I knew he would be there but I had a thought of what was I to do if he wasn't at the station because I was in a strange country now. We shook hands and Mr. Jackson told me his shoe shop was on Moore Street three blocks from the Train Depot. We walked to the shop, then he told me that I could stay with him until I get a place of my own. The shop was small and reminded me Papa's shop in Odessa.

It was not nearly as large as the Justin Boot Factory but then Mr. Jackson didn't make many boots and shoes, he mainly repaired them. He told me that the brick buildings around the Depot were all new. It seems that in 1895, one or two train cars exploded one night, leveling and burning most of the downtown area. Most of the buildings were wooden and burned very quickly. The Santa Fe Railroad paid for all the damage and most of the wooden buildings had been replaced with brick. I asked if anyone was killed in the explosion and he didn't answer so I didn't bring up the subject again.

Chapter Twelve
A New Life in Oklahoma

The Jackson Shoe Shop was well organized. It was in a two-story building and Mr. Jackson said that he lived upstairs. He had a large sign over his door and a window with displays of boots and shoes that he could make and a display of repairs on boots and shoes. My two satchels were put in the back and the box with Mama's oil lamp was put on my workbench. There were several pairs of boots that he had started to repair and told me he had too much work for one person. He then put his hand on top of my box and asked, "What have you got in here?" I opened the box and took out Mama's oil lamp and told him the story. He said it was a good possession and to be careful with it. I put it back in the box and moved it to a corner of the workbench. He asked if I could help him now because several men would be coming back for their boots. I said of course and the rest of the day and into the evening I helped him repair the boots on the bench. We did take a break to eat a small supper at a local restaurant then went back to work. We finished about 7:00 p.m. and he told me he that he was glad I was in his shop now.

One thing I'll always remember is Mr. Westheimer coming to the shop. He had come from New York City on his way to Texas but he stopped in Ardmore in 1890 and went into business with Samuel Daube in The Blue Front Store. He was a very distinguished looking gentleman and introduced himself and said he heard that I was new in town and came to welcome me. In our conversation he told me about the Jewish community there being the first in Oklahoma. He also said they had organized Temple Emeth, Hebrew for Truth, and were planning to build a synagogue. When he left several other members came to the shop. Mr. Jackson told me that Mr. Westheimer and Mr. Daube were the lead-ers of the Jewish community in Ardmore and in fact they had both been instrumental in establishing Temple Emeth. They told Mr. Jackson that the first Jewish community in Oklahoma was in Ardmore, not Tulsa or Oklahoma City as one would expect. The community was organized while Ardmore was still in Indian Territory.

I wanted to ask if he was married and where his wife was and just as I was thinking about this he told me that his wife had died in the fire from the railroad explosion and they had no children. This explained why he didn't answer when I asked if anyone had been killed in the explosion and fire. I never brought up the subject again. We went upstairs and he had a spare room for me that was nicely furnished. Most of the furniture looked new and I suspected he had purchased it when I agreed to come to his shop. I unpacked Mama's oil lamp and put it on a small stand, then unpacked my two satchels. He called me and I went to the living room in the front of the building and he asked me to sit down. It was explained that Ardmore was a rough town and the oil field workers could be a fiery bunch, especially when they came to town on Saturday Night when they were drinking. I told him that I don't think I would be out on Saturday night.

He said he and his wife had come from Memphis, Tennessee, to Ardmore in 1893, six years after it had been established. He explained that it was a much rougher town in those days and it was not unusual for a body to be lying in the street each morning. It was a rough town until statehood in 1907. Before statehood, the town was divided between two US Marshals, and they didn't interfere with each other. After statehood, a city police force was established and things started to settle down. I was then told that the Jewish community kept to themselves and didn't take part in the rowdiness of Ardmore, especially on the Sabbath. This impressed me and then I asked about the Civilized Indians in Ardmore. He chuckled and told me the Chickasaw Indians were one of the Five Civilized Indian Tribes that been brought from the east in the 1830s and were called civilized because they had adopted the white way, but it didn't mean they were not civilized. He continued the conversation and told me to be careful when I went out and what part of town I went too. There was a section of town where the oil field workers went that the respectable people didn't go. I assured him that I would not go to that section of town but I would appreciate it if he would show me this section to avoid. He laughed and said it would be good if I knew where not to go. He added that the Ku Klux Klan had a group in the Ardmore area but were not too active. I had heard of the KKK in Texas, but nothing had happened. He explained they were against the Blacks, Catholics and Jews, and he warned me again to be careful but Mr. Westheimer and Mr. Daube could tell me much more than he could. He said it was getting late and time for bed but he always had one drink before he retired and asked if I would join him. I said I would and explained that I was not a heavy drinker and he told me he knew that. We had our drink and I retired to my room and was thinking of my life at this point, and about leaving Texas and coming to Oklahoma to Ardmore, which Mr. Jackson described as a frontier town.

The work in the Jackson Shoe Shop was good and I was busy. I paid $10.00 a month for room and board with Mr. Jackson. He had a good business and after one month, he gave me a raise to $10.00 a week. This was more money that I had ever made in my life. Families would come in to have new shoes made for their children when they had outgrown the old ones. I knew this was a good shop if families came in. There were very few children's shoes to be repaired because they outgrew them so fast. Mr. Jackson said he made the shoes for the children at the end of the summer when they were preparing to go back to school. He made all the new boots and shoes and I was kept busy repairing work boots. One man brought several boots in to be repaired from the oil field and he must have been a foreman or something. I never really talked to him since Mr. Jackson always dealt with him and I repaired the boots he brought to the shop. I felt I didn't have the freedom I had in Fort Worth. Some of the people I met seemed to be mistrustful of me because I still had my Russian accent. I didn't go out much and when I did it was with Mr. Jackson or to the temple. We prepared most of our meals but always went to temple for the beginning of the Sabbath.

The people at the synagogue were wonderful. I was invited to their homes and one boy saw my tattoo and asked what it was. I was hesitant and Mr. Daube mentioned the tattoo that he had seen it before while I was working at the temple one day. He didn't say anything but I knew he was aware that Jews were not allowed to have any tattoos. I explained about the Self Defense in Odessa and the word spread like wildfire among the community. I couldn't comprehend that knowledge of the Self Defense

This is the first synagogue in Ardmore. This has been the First Christian Church and we purchased the building. I got this photo from the Ardmore Library.

had spread all the way to Ardmore, Oklahoma. Several stories were relayed to me about the Jewish community. I was told Samuel Zuckerman was the first Jew that came to Ardmore and he arrived on the train in 1888 and established a general store. I was also told that Ike Fisherman came to the US through Galveston and got off the train in Ardmore and began peddling bananas then went into the scrap metal business. I met Jews from Germany, Russia, Romania, and even France. Ardmore sure had a thriving Jewish community. We had services and Rabbi George Fox came from Fort Worth once in a while to lead the services.

I was glad to be busy and Mr. Jackson gave me a raise to $10.50 a week and I was able to put money in the bank. Mr. Jackson had a small safe in the shop and once a week he paid me then took the money to the bank. I always went with him and put a little in my account. The people at the bank were always friendly and one young man always talked to me. One day he told me he enjoyed talking to me because he liked my accent and we had many good conversations. He was not Jewish and that did not seem to matter. I realized this was a great country because in Russia I would have never had conversations like this with someone that was not Jewish.

I had been in Ardmore for almost six months and Mr. Jackson had hired another worker, John to help in the shop. He had to hire another worker because the business was still growing. He had been in the shop for almost two months and was a good worker and we had become friends. He had come from a shoe shop in Dallas to work for Mr. Jackson. He was a young man and seemed to enjoy Ardmore. One morning Mr. Jackson said he was taking some boots and shoes to Tulsa, which was in northeast Oklahoma. He wanted me to accompany him and that John could watch the store. It seems there was to be a meeting of shoemakers in Tulsa and Mr. Jackson wanted to attend. The meeting was in one month and he asked if I could make a pair of boots as I had in Odessa to take to Tulsa and I agreed. It took about two and a half weeks to finish the boots and Mr. Jackson was very pleased with them. He had made several pairs of shoes and was also taking several pairs of boots I had made. He told me the trip to Tulsa would take one full day, the meeting would be two days then one day to return. We would be gone four days and John said he could watch the shop with no problem. I told Mr. Daube that I was going to Tulsa with Mr. Jackson and he told me Tulsa was a good city.

We left the next week and the trip was very pleasant. We stopped in all the small towns and everyone seemed to be friendly. The two towns I remember were Seminole and Okmulgee. When we arrived we took rooms at the Alexander Hotel in downtown Tulsa. Tulsa was a beautiful city situated on the Arkansas River. The meeting started the next day at the Brady Hotel and we were putting out the boots in a display with other shoemakers from Oklahoma, Arkansas and Missouri.

Mr. Jackson attended the meetings and I met the people that came to the displays. A man stopped by and picked up one of the boots I had made. It was one of the boots as I had made in Russia. He turned the boot over in his hands and said this is a very fine boot. He asked if I had made it and I told him, yes. He asked where I was from and I told him Ardmore. He said I was not from Ardmore because of my accent, then I told him I had come from Odessa, Russia, and this was the type of boot I made for sailors in the Black Sea Fleet. He asked how long I had been making boots and I told him I had been a shoemaker for my father in Russia because he had been a shoemaker. He put the boot down and walked away.

He returned after a short while and introduced himself as Charles Burns and he had a shoe shop in Tulsa. He explained that Tulsa was just beginning to really grow and he wanted a good boot maker. He asked what I was making in Ardmore and I didn't tell him. I told him that I couldn't leave Mr. Jackson because I had only been with him six months. He explained that Tulsa was on the move because the Glenpool Oil Field had been brought in and this would be a good opportunity. I asked where his shop was and he told me right across from the Brady Hotel. He gave me his address and telephone number and left. When Mr. Jackson returned I told him what had transpired. He told me if I could get a good salary from Mr. Burns to take it. He said Ardmore was no place for a young man like me, and that I should be in a big city. The next day Mr. Burns returned and I hailed him. I introduced him to Mr. Jackson and Mr. Burns said he wanted to hire me. Mr. Jackson put his hand on my shoulder and said he was paying me $12.00 a week and he would have to do better than that. I wanted to say I was only making $10.50 but didn't. Mr. Burns said he could give me $13.50 a week and Mr. Jackson said I should take it. We shook hands and Mr. Burns asked if I still had the address, even though it was right across from the hotel. I took out the paper and showed him. He then asked when I could begin work and Mr. Jackson asked if I wanted to return to Ardmore or should he send my things to me. I quickly said I had to return to Ardmore to ensure I got Mama's oil lamp. Mr. Burns told me he would give me one week to be in his shop then he left. He returned and said he would have a train ticket waiting for me at the depot in Ardmore. After he left I asked Mr. Jackson why he said I was making $12.00 a week and he said he wanted to make sure I had a good wage because Tulsa would be more expensive.

The meeting closed and we headed back to Ardmore. I thanked Mr. Jackson for what he had done for me. He said it was just a matter of time before something happened. Even though there was a Jewish population in Ardmore, there were still a few problems now and then. Mr. Westhiemer and Mr. Daube always told us to stay away from trouble.

If we did go out we always made sure we did not go alone and if there was trouble to just walk away

I packed my two satchels and Mama's oil lamp and went downstairs and said my good byes to John. The door opened and several people that I had made boots and shoes for came in to tell me goodbye. I had not made many friends in Ardmore outside of the temple except several people I made shoes for and the teller at the bank. Mr. Jackson went me to the bank and I withdrew the $40.00 I had in my account. I told the young teller I was moving to Tulsa and he said he was sorry to see me go. From the bank we walked to the temple. I told them I was moving to Tulsa and it seemed everyone was there to say goodbye. I had told Mr. Jackson I had to stop at the temple before going to the train station. Mr. Jackson walked with me to the station with several people from the temple. It was kind of sad, I was just beginning to make friends and I was leaving again. We walked and I don't think we said one word. My ticket to Tulsa was waiting. I looked at the ticket and the date was February 15th, 1915. My life was changing so very fast from Russia to Dallas to Fort Worth to Ardmore and now to Tulsa. Mr. Westheimer said he was sorry to see me leave as did Mr. Daube. They left and Mr. Jackson and I shook hands and he told me I was a good boot maker. I boarded the train and headed back to Tulsa and what seemed a new beginning.

I felt more secure. I had money in my pocket, $40.00, and I hailed a taxi and gave him the address of the Burns Shoe Shop across the street from the Brady Hotel. I stepped out of the taxi with my two satchels and Mama's oil lamp and Mr. Burns came to the door and said he was very pleased I was there. He told me that he was spreading the word that he was getting a new boot maker that had experience in making a good work boot. The first thing I had to do was get settled. Mr. Burns told me of a rooming house on Main Street and he took me there and a room had been reserved for me. The landlord was Mr. Toalson and the apartment had two rooms and I shared a bath with the other four apartments on the floor. The rent was $20.00 a month and I agreed and moved in. This was also furnished and Mr. Burns gave me the rest of the day to get unpacked and to be at work in the morning at 8:00. I asked him where the nearest bank was and he took me to the First National Bank and I opened an account with $10.00. I kept $10.00 for food and incidentals. I was too excited to rest and went out for a walk. Tulsa was a booming city. I walked downtown past the Alexander and Brady Hotels. Two fine hotels in Tulsa. I stopped at a small café and had a bite to eat, then returned to my apartment. I went to bed and was ready for work the next morning.

The Burns Shoe Shop was within walking distance and after having breakfast at the same café, I walked through the door just before 8:00. Mr. Burns told me it was good to be punctual. That first day I worked on several pairs of boots that been brought in. I was introduced to many, many customers and knew this was going to be a good life. I had been at the shop just a few weeks and was repairing boots for the farmers and ranchers in the Tulsa area. More people were moving to Tulsa and the business increased and I was given a raise to $15.00 a week. Many of our customers were staying across the street in the Brady Hotel and came to our shop. Word spread that I made a good boot and the business increased more. One boot that became popular was the style of boot I had made for the sailors in the Black Sea Fleet. Mr. Burns had me make a pair and he put them in the shop window.

I met several Jewish families in Tulsa and even visited their homes. Tulsa didn't have a Synagogue and we met in homes and Mr. Aaronson held many of the services in his home. I was told the first services were held above the office of Mr. Livingston on Elgin Street. We met in different homes and I became acquainted with most of the Jewish community. This brought back memories of Roshen when the Rabbi would come to our home. Rabbi Raab had arrived in Tulsa just before Hannakkah of 1914 from St. Louis, so we did have a Rabbi in Tulsa. It felt good to have these people around and be in a bigger city. I had felt alone in Ardmore but Tulsa was much better.

After about two months, Mr. Cox came into the shop. He lived in Boynton, a small town near Muskogee and came to Tulsa on a regular basis and brought all of his boots and shoes to Mr. Burns. Mr. Cox was Creek Indian and the land on which he lived was his allotment. His son lived in Tulsa and he said he was getting too old to live on the farm and was preparing to move to Tulsa. We became friends and I asked him one day if he was still considering selling his farm and he answered, yes. I told him that I always wanted to be an American farmer and would be interested in buying his farm, but I would have to pay it out. He said that was no problem because he didn't need much money to live on. Mr. Burns spoke for me and we struck a deal where I was to buy his farm after I went out to inspect it. It was a beautiful farm with a small house and he was asking $500.00 for the 180 acres. I only had $60.00 in the bank but told Mr. Cox that I'm sure I could get the money from my Uncle Herman in Dallas. I sent a telegraph to Uncle Herman and told him I wanted to do. He sent a telegram and agreed to loan me half the money for the farm, which would be $250.00. Mr. Cox said that would be fine and I could pay rest out. We had the papers drawn up that I would pay $10.00 a month until the farm was paid off. With interest, the farm would be paid off in three years. We signed the papers and I was an American farmer.

The shoe shop was doing a good business and I was making my payments to Mr. Cox and a telegram arrived from the McMann Oil Company in Tulsa. I didn't recognize the name of the company but there were dozens of oil companies in Tulsa now. The telegram stated they wanted to lease the farm to explore for oil. I asked Mr. Cox and he said the oil companies were drilling the area and finding oil. I met with the representatives of the oil company and signed the papers. I made enough money on the oil lease to pay off the farm. I contacted Mr. Cox and paid him in full. He was glad that I was doing so well and wished me luck.

Work continued and I was repairing boots and making new ones, then everything changed. It was just a month or two later they struck oil on the farm. The first well was bringing in over 300 barrels a day and more wells were being drilled. The money came in, deposited in my bank account and I couldn't believe what was happening. Mr. Burns told me how happy he was for me. I went to bed that night thinking of how great it was to be in America and in Tulsa, Oklahoma. It was hard to fathom how my life had changed from Roshen to Oklahoma and wondered what was over the horizon

The sun looked the same, Tulsa looked the same, but I felt different. I felt more secure. I was having money deposited in the bank and it felt good. I had never had money like this before. The first thing I did was to pay Uncle Herman back the money he loaned me. I then thought that I wanted to stay the same person. I didn't want to become someone else. Mr. Burns told me that he knew several people who had come into money and their life changed completely. Some began acting like they were better than others and even looked down on some old friends. Some had frittered their money away and were right back where they started. I was not going to act like that. After all, I was just an immigrant from Russia. I thought back to Galveston when I had 75 cents to my name when I got off the boat, and having to borrow money to get through customs was humiliating, but I survived. I was determined to remember where I had come from and that I was going to continue trying to repay what I had gained in America. In just over three years I had gone from 75 cents in my pocket to making $35.00 a day in oil royalties and working at the shoe shop. It seemed like a miracle.

Tulsa was becoming a boomtown. I met some customers that lived in Sapulpa. There was a shoe shop in Sapulpa, but they liked Mr. Burns much better. They said that Sapulpa had been the railhead and was much larger than Tulsa. A hotel was needed but Sapulpa didn't build one and Tulsa did. Because of this hotel, all the people began to shift to Tulsa and people moved and Sapulpa stopped growing. It was a nice town and I have often wondered if that hotel had been built, what type of city would Sapulpa be. I'm sure it would be the huge city and Tulsa would just small village. But that didn't happen. There was also a good-sized Jewish community in Tulsa, but we had no Synagogue. My first task was to set about having one built. I had enough money to help start the Synagogue but I wanted the whole community to join in the project. With the whole community involved, everyone could take pride in the Temple. Rabbi Raab already had plans to build a Temple and now we could raise money and hire an architect. With the oil boom in progress, and with Tulsa growing as fast as it was, more people were arriving and the Jewish population was increasing.

The Jewish population had increased and even I couldn't believe it. In 1914, Temple Israel was established in Tulsa under the leadership of Abraham Feldman and we rented space from the Knights of Columbus to hold our services. Jews renting from Christians to hold services would have never happened in Russia. This made my belief in Tulsa and America much stronger and I was glad I was here. Temple Israel finally built the synagogue in 1919 and on the first Sabbath meeting after it was completed a group from the Knights of Columbus was invited. I wondered again, a group of Christians in the temple on the Sabbath, this would have never happed in Russia either. It was a good dedication and the whole community came together. There was only one problem, Temple Israel was reformed and I wanted an orthodox synagogue, as did several other men in the community.

I sent Mr. Cox $10.00 and told him that I felt I owed him the money because of what had happened. Two days later, he came into the shop and gave the money back to me. He said he respected me but the land was mine and he didn't believe in taking handouts. He then said there are more important things in life than money. He then said he decided not to move to Tulsa but had moved into Boynton. I told him that I would like to pay his fare back to Boynton and he said I could do that. I gave him $10.00 to pay for the trip and he took it. He said this was not a handout, this was fare money. We shook hands and as he was leaving, he turned and said that I was a good man and good things were coming my way. He even called me a friend to the Indians. Mr. Burns told me that he was impressed with what I had done and repeated that good things would be coming to me.

Business increased with the influx of oil workers. Some of the boots that were brought in to be repaired couldn't be repaired. The boots were soaked through with oil and many were ripped and torn. I did my best to repair the boots and the ones that couldn't be repaired, I handed back. I thought work in the oil fields must be rough. I heard and read in the newspaper of the men that were killed and injured on these oil rigs. These workers could not afford a new pair of boots. I knew this and asked Mr. Burns if I could make new boots for them and let them pay it out. He hesitated and said he had never done this. I then offered to pay for the boots then the workers could pay me back. He agreed to this because he said he had never sold on credit before and didn't want to start now. At one time, I had 15 pairs of boots that I had made and purchased and the workers were paying me. The result of this was the business in the shop almost doubled. Mr. Burns thanked me for what I had done then paid me for all the money I had out and he began selling boots on credit. I don't know of one single worker that did not pay for his boots. I recall several men coming back years later and paying for the boots they had purchased on credit. Mr. Burns even had to hire two more people in the shop to keep up with the business. He hired Tom Johnson as a clerk to keep up with all the paperwork.

Chapter Thirteen

Tulsa and the Race Massacre

The war was raging in Europe and I was worried about Mama and Papa. Russia had many troops in the conflict. I was afraid that Simon would be called up. I received a letter from Mama and she told me that Simon had died. Simon, my younger brother was dead. The next day I received a telegram for Solomon telling me the same news and he wanted to make sure that I knew about Simon. Part of my world had died. I would never see Simon again and I thought back to the times in Russia when Simon was born and how we played together but now he was gone.

Rabbi Raab had a memorial service for Simon and Mr. Burns even gave me several days off. I wrote to Mama and told her the grief I felt and asked how she and the girls were doing. I received more devastating news. Papa had died. My world was falling apart. Solomon sent a telegram and wanted to come to Tulsa. He arrived in three days and we sat and talked about the times in Russia and Papa and Simon. I told him that I was thinking about returning to Russia since I was the oldest and should take over the family. He asked how I could think of going back. He said that Mama was moving to Poland. Gueti had married a man from Warsaw and moved to Poland. Gueti and her husband had invited Mama and Rosa to come to Warsaw and live with them.

I wrote Mama in Warsaw and told her how I felt and she wrote back very quickly and told me not to return because I had a good life in America and there was nothing I could do in Russia. There was no family left in Russia and I would be an outsider in Poland. She explained there was a very large Jewish community in Warsaw and things were going very well. She just wished that Papa and Simon could be with her. She went on to explain how much better everything was in Warsaw than in Russia. She told me to stay to watch after Solomon. I knew I didn't have to look after Solomon, he was doing very well on his own. With Mama's last letter I decided to stay in America. It would have been difficult to return and give up everything in Tulsa. I don't think Mama realized how large America was. She wanted me to look after Solomon and I lived in Tulsa. Where Mama lived, that would have been half way across Europe.

The price of oil went up as the demand rose for the war effort. I didn't feel right. I was making more money because of the war and the suffering it was causing. During the first Liberty Bond Drive, I bought several hundred dollars in bonds. There was even talk of the United States getting involved in the war. I would fight for America. But my underlying question was why was there a war in the first place. I had lived in Germany and made many friends. Why were the Czar and the Kaiser fighting? I thought back to the pogrom in Odessa. I had driven those thoughts from my mind because those were not happy memories. To contemplate that the killing may spread across Europe was unthinkable. My family and my memories were in Europe. The newspaper stories about the destruction in Belgium and the fighting in France brought back the memories of the pogrom and I wept.

The war affected my work. I was still making good boots but Mr. Burns noticed. We talked about the war and I even told him of the pogrom in Odessa and he tried to understand but war and pogroms are senseless. I wanted to take all of my money and buy world peace. There were several boys from Tulsa that went to Canada and joined the Canadian Army. The war seemed to be getting closer. The bright spot was money was coming in for another Synagogue, this one was to be orthodox, B'nai Emunah.

A bank account was opened and I was making a weekly contribution. An architect was hired and we bought a lot at 9th and Cheyenne Streets just south of downtown on which the Synagogue was to be built. The building went up very fast and was made of the finest oak and walnut. There was always a group watching the construction and some members were even helping the builders. It wasn't as grand as the Synagogues in Fort Worth or Odessa or even Temple Israel in Tulsa but it was ours. I paid for a Star of David that was placed in the top of the gable that faced the street. The building was 30 feet wide and 70 feet long and was dedicated in May of 1916. People came from miles around for the dedication. Rabbi Blat came from Oklahoma City with a new Torah for the tabernacle. It was a grand ceremony and the food was wonderful. Bishop Meershcart of the Catholic Church and Bishop Brooke of the Episcopal Church came and Rabbi Raab had a wonderful, beautiful service. We now had two Synagogues in Tulsa.

The Jewish community was growing in Tulsa as the city grew. In fact a chapter of the National Council of Jewish Women was established in Tulsa in 1917. Tulsa was the

This is the original Temple Israel in Tulsa.

fastest growing city in America. Families were moving here everyday to work in the oil fields and new oil companies were being developed and opening headquarters in Tulsa. Mr. Burns even hired another man, Jim Davis, to work in the shoe shop and it was booming just like the oil fields.

April came and America entered the war. I wanted to enlist but couldn't for two reasons. I was too old and I wasn't a citizen. I was 29 years old and knew I had to become an American citizen, I owed this much to America. I bought Liberty bonds on a weekly basis and so many boys from Tulsa were going to the service. The draft was getting most of them and others were joining the Navy and the Marines. Mr. Burns even repaired boots and shoes for boys that were going into the service.

Our clerk, Tom Johnson received his draft notice and Sarah Thomason was hired to take his place. I noticed that women were now doing many of the jobs in town because so many of the boys had gone to war. Whenever possible I went to the train station to see the boys off and Mr. Burns went with me when he could. There was always a crowd of people at the station along with the families of the boys leaving. A lot of the oil field workers were joining the service and some joined in Tulsa and some went back to their homes to join. We had several boys from the community go to the service and we always had a send off for them. Then the telegrams began arriving of the boys from Tulsa that had been killed or wounded. The customers that had boys in the service were terrified of getting one of those telegrams and several did. There was nothing anyone could say to them.

I felt as if I were not doing my part. The oil kept coming in and the war was dragging on and I kept buying war bonds. Then I read in the newspaper that Russia was dropping out of the war and Russia was on the verge of a revolution. The Czar had tried to bring about reforms and even abdicated and a democratic republic had been organized under Alexander Kerensky. That government lasted only about a year and the Bolsheviks fomented a revolution and took over the government in 1918. A man named Lenin had taken over and the Czar and his entire family had been executed in July of 1918. I was not a fan of the Czar but to kill him and his entire family was absurd. What was Russia coming too? Russia was now a whole lifetime away and I didn't want to dwell on it.

The war ended and Armistice Day in Tulsa was beyond description. All the boys were coming home and perhaps everything could get back to normal. Of course the families that had lost boys in the war could never get back to normal. Tom Johnson came home and took his job as clerk and Miss Thomason had to be let go and she was not happy. She enjoyed working and was determined to find another job. Business in the shop picked up. The boys were back in the oil fields but not as much oil was needed as during the war. There was also a change in Tulsa. A lot of the boys that came back from France were different. They had been gone away excited young men and came back weary old men even though some were barely twenty years old. The war changed them.

More changes were about to happen. Mr. Burns told me he was ready to get out of the shoe business. He asked if I would be interested in taking over his shop and I immediately said yes. I worked out a plan to buy the Brady Shoe Shop. I had $500 in liberty bonds and signed them over to Mr. Burns then would pay $150.00 a month and in one year the shop would be paid off and be mine. Business at the shop was slowing down because there was a depression after the war. I had to let Tom Johnson go and I took over his duties as clerk. Another man quit and I can't remember his name. He went to the oil fields where he was going to work on boots in a portable shoe shop. I had to have another worker. Two workers were gone and we still had a lot of business.

Most of our work now was repairing boots and shoes because people couldn't buy new ones. I put an advertisement in the paper and Henry Brown came in to apply. He knew his shoes and I hired him. He lived in the Greenwood area of Tulsa and was black. He made a good shoe and was good at repairing so I didn't care what color he was. Jim and Henry worked good together and the shop was doing good.

There were rough looking characters on the streets of Tulsa in those days and one came into the shop. He was dressed like he was used to hard work and asked if I was Louis Kerbel. I told him I was and he introduced himself. I can't remember his name but he was someone like Tom Slick. He was a wildcatter and wanted to drill his own wells. He told me he had been working in the oil fields and had enough money to buy a drilling rig but didn't have pipe. He was told that there was oil on my place and wanted me to help him out. I told him I didn't have any pipe but I knew a man that did. His name was Sam Wasserman and dealt

This is a photograph of the Kerbel Shoe Shop.. It is just a Xerox copy because I lost the original photo.

in scrap metal. He drove a horse and wagon and gathered up scrap metal around Tulsa and bought all kinds of junk. Oil companies were coming and going because they were not all successful.

I told Mr. Slick, or whatever his name was that if anyone knew where to get pipe, Sam would. I told him where Sam had his junk yard and off he went. Well Sam told me later that he struck a deal with this guy. He did have drill pipe and let him have with the condition that if he struck oil, he wanted one fourth of the well if oil was found and if no oil was found, he would simply return the pipe. They agreed and this guy took the pipe and headed northwest of Tulsa to Pawhuska and worked with a guy named Marland and they discovered the Burbank Oil Field. Well the rest is history. Sam had a one-fourth interest in this oil well and that is how he got his start. He sure doesn't have to collect junk anymore.

With the Glenpool and Burbank Oil Fields both in production, Tulsa was booming. New buildings were being built and work in the shop was picking up. I had three workers in the shop and I bought electric machines and put the old treadle machines in storage in the back of the shop. The electric machines made the work so much easier and we could get more done. But some people thought Tulsa was growing too fast so that law and order couldn't keep up with the growth.

During all these time, I still thought of Russia and the pogrom was still in the back of my mind. I tried to suppress those memories but they kept coming back, especially at night. I had met Roy Belton who was a young man in the community that worked for the telephone company. He had been in the shop and seemed like a nice young man. In August of 1920 he was accused of shooting Homer Nida, a taxi driver in Tulsa. The driver was badly wounded by a gunshot and identified Roy as the man that shot him. Roy was taken to jail and after Homer died on the 28th of August, a mob went to the jail, took him out of his cell, drove several miles south of town and lynched him.

Sheriff Gustafson said he tried to prevent the mob but how did a mob get him out of a locked cell on the top floor of the Tulsa jail, put him in a car and drive south of town without the police knowing? There were reports that the police even directed traffic around the scene of the lynching. I don't know if Roy shot the man or not but a trial should have decided his fate, not a lynch mob. This devastated the whole community. America had been so good to me and now this. All I could think of was the pogrom in Odessa and how the police did nothing to prevent or stop it. I didn't know what to do. America was the land of opportunity and didn't have pogroms and shouldn't have lynchings. I prayed to God this didn't happen again. But man's inhumanity to man raised its ugly head in Tulsa again. It was the 31st of May in 1921.

The Drexel Building was on Main Street, one block from Archer and it seems that Dick Rowland, a young black man worked in a shoe-shine shop. I knew many of the people that worked in the shine shops because we were all in the shoe business. The day was normal and business was good. Jim Davis and Henry didn't show up and I wondered why because they had always been on time. About 10:00 that morning Henry ran into the shop and yelled, "Mr. Kerbel, hide me, they are killing us!" I asked what was going on and he said that Dick Rowland had been arrested for assaulting a white woman in the elevator of the Drexel Building and a lynch mob was going to hang him. He told me that he knew Dick didn't do it but they were going to hang him. He also said a group of blacks said they had enough and were also forming mobs to stop the lynching.

I thought of Roy Belton and said, "My God, not again!" I saw a group of white men breaking into a gun shop and taking the guns and ammunition. All I could think of was a pogrom in Tulsa. I told Henry to go upstairs and be quiet.

There was a balcony in the shop where I kept supplies and used as a storage area. At this moment Mr. Bishop came into my shop with two blacks that worked for him. He owned a café and told me he had no place to hide his workers and told them to go upstairs where Henry was and be quite. None of the three had families in Tulsa we had to worry about. I heard gunfire and noises and shouting and all I could do was cry. Everything came flooding back.

I went to the front of the store and saw smoke coming from the Greenwood area. It looked like it was being burned and the smoke looked like Odessa. I saw Jim running with a rifle. He came to the front of the store out of breath. I asked, "Jim, what are you doing?" He said, "Henry is a nigger and I'm going to kill him!" I looked at his eyes and I had seen those eyes in the mob in Odessa. I said, "Jim, yesterday you and Henry were friends." I knew he wasn't thinking straight because the mob mentality is like a cattle stampede. When it begins, all rationality is forgotten.

I stood in the door and told him to go home, that Henry wasn't here, he didn't come to work today. He looked at me and I sternly told him to go home and cool down, you don't know what you are doing! He looked at me and a hint of recognition came over his face. He then ran away still carrying his rifle. Police cars were racing by, people were running and shops were closing or hadn't even opened. I heard more gunfire and breaking glass and saw more smoke. I stood in the doorway and was not leaving. I was not going to let this happen. I was going to stay and protect my friends. This time they were going to have to kill me. Every time I heard a gunshot I jumped and thought of Odessa.

I saw some soldiers coming down the street heading toward Greenwood. Jim came by the shop again and I told him Henry still wasn't here. I stood in my shop most of the day and the noise rose and fell. I went to the stairs and called out, "Henry, it's me, Louis!" I walked up the stairs and all three were lying on the floor. I told them that I was going to Mr. Bishop's restaurant and get some food and not to move. I walked out, locked the door and walked to the restaurant. The door was locked and the curtain closed. I knocked and Mr. Bishop peeked from behind the curtain and opened the door then locked it again. He said he locked the door when two men came in looking for the blacks that worked there. I could see the hurt in his eyes and told him that I was hungry and could I get something to eat. He said sure.

There were several of his workers in the place and I told him that I was really hungry and had not eaten all day. He understood and made some sandwiches and stacked them on a tray. He put a cloth over them and I pulled the cloth off. I wanted to make sure everyone knew I was carrying sandwiches on this tray. I returned to the shop, opened the door and went to the stairs and called out to Henry again. I took the tray upstairs then went down and got three glasses of water and took upstairs. I sat on the floor and talked about the pogrom in Russia and what I had gone through.

Henry said, "Then you have seen this before." I said I had and didn't understand. I began crying and Henry crawled over to me and put his arms around me. He said, "Mr. Kerbel, I'm sorry you have to go through this again." I said, "I'm sorry you have to go through this for the first time, what is going to happen to Tulsa? I don't think Odessa ever recovered and I don't think Tulsa will ever recover from this." I told them in Russia it was hate because we were Jews and blamed for losing the war with Japan but here it was hate because of a man's skin color and I didn't understand this.

I went back downstairs and to keep my mind busy I worked on a pair of boots but it was mindless work. I didn't pay any attention to what I was doing. It was just something to do. Henry called from upstairs. He said they had to go to the toilet. We had one in the back of the shop. I went to the front door and looked out. I didn't see anyone and told Henry and the coast was clear. I kept watch while all three came down then returned to the balcony.

I saw more soldiers coming down the street and things seemed to get quiet. I was in the door of my shop and two stopped and asked if this was my shop and told them it was and I was the owner. They said the governor had called out the National Guard to stop the riot and they were gathering blacks to take to the baseball field for protection. They were to take any black for their own protection. I thought the three had done pretty well in the balcony and said there were no blacks in the shop. It was dark and I closed the shop and locked the door. I then went up stairs and spent the night in the balcony. It was a fitful night. None of us slept. The next morning I opened the shop and saw soldiers patrolling the street. I asked how everything was going and they told me the riot had been stopped. I asked are you sure and they said yes that they had orders to shoot to kill any looters. They asked if I was going to open the shop and I said I was. They said nothing else was opened and I said I wanted something to be normal and it was normal for me to open my shop.

I called up to the three and told them everything was over. They peered down from the balcony and a soldier asked how long they had been up there. I told them since yesterday and that I didn't let them go to the baseball field because I wanted to make sure they were safe. They came down the stairs and still had fear in their eyes. The soldiers said they could go home, if their homes were still there, that most of the Greenwood area had been burned out. The soldiers had a truck and offered to take Henry and the other to the baseball field. They wanted to see if their homes were still there and Henry asked if I would go with them. I said of course.

We drove through the Greenwood area and I had been through it many times but I didn't recognize one thing. I looked just like Odessa. Henry's apartment house had been burned and the homes of the other two had also been burned. Henry said he had no place to stay and I told him he could stay with me that I had plenty of room. I told the other two they could also stay with me that we would make out somehow bur Mr. Bishop took them in.

The community collected clothes for people that had been burned out and some families even took in families that had been burned out. Henry stayed with me four months until he found a place. His family came for a visit from Okmulgee and his brother took my hand and told me that if I ever needed anything to let him know because I was a friend for life for saving his brother. I told him that I knew what a riot was, that I had gone through the same thing in Russia. I said that I was just glad to help in some way in the middle of all this madness, death and destruction.

After everything was over, the official report said that 39 people had been killed but I had been told that more than 2,000 had been killed because it was a race war not a race riot. Almost the entire Greenwood area had been burned and would never recover. This was a sad time in my life. Thinking America was such a great county. I was determined this was never going to happen in my town again.

Chapter Fourteen
Striking Oil

Things began to return to normal very slowly. Jim came by to the shop. I looked at him and said, "Leave this shop right now and don't you ever come back!" I never saw him again. I don't know if he left Tulsa or what happened and I really didn't care. Henry stayed with me and was a true and trusted friend. There were open wounds in Tulsa that would take generations to heal if they ever healed. After the riot, business dropped everywhere. Jim Evans came into the shop about two weeks after the riot. He had owned a shoe shop in the Greenwood area. He had been in my shop many times and I had been in his shop and we helped each other out. He came looking for work. He had been burned out and lost everything, his shop and his home but all of his family survived because he had fled Tulsa when the trouble started. He had three employees and they had lost everything. Jim was about 60 years old and said he was too old to start over again and didn't know what he was going to do. He stood in my shop and began crying. I said, "Jim, I'll make you a deal. I have some old equipment that I don't need anymore. I just bought some new machines and have some old machines in the back that are still good and if you want them to reopen your shop you can have them."

I took him to the back and showed him the treadle machines and explained they were just taking up space. He looked at me with tears in his eyes. I told Henry to watch the store. We loaded the machines in the back of my pickup truck and drove to his old store. The walls were standing but had been gutted by the fire. Two of his employees were there cleaning out the store and we unloaded the machines. I saw the skeletons of the old machines among the rubble and we pushed them out of the building and brought in my old machines. I told him these were his now and I would help him with whatever he needed. I loaned him money to rebuild his store. I told him to rebuild the store and reopen it and to "get back on your feet, then you can think about paying the money back." He paid back every penny. Jim Evans was a good friend of mine and he made a good shoes also. As I drove back to the shop, I looked at the burned-out houses and businesses. People were milling around and soldiers were still patrolling the streets. The cleanup effort had begun but it was going to take a long time.

Tulsa continued to grow but only after the Greenwood affair had been cleaned up and a lot of families left Tulsa. The oil boom continued and the business in my shop returned. One day in April of 1925, a young lady brought a pair of shoes into the shop to be repaired. She had a pretty face that I had not seen before. I looked at her as she explained that she wanted half soles on her shoes. Our eyes met and she glanced down very quickly. I wrote down her name, "Elizabeth Waldron," and told her the shoes would be ready tomorrow and she left. Henry asked, "Tomorrow?" You have a lot of work before you start on those shoes. I told Henry that for that face I would start on her shoes. The rest of the day I worked on her shoes and thought of her face. She was a bright spot. She returned at 10:00 the next morning and picked up her shoes. I told her that I had not seen her before and she said she had just taken a job with Mr. Skelly in his oil company and when asked about a shoe shop, my name was mentioned. She came back and asked if I could make a new pair of shoes for her. I said, "of course," and invited her to the back of the store. She sat in a chair and I measured each foot and she did have pretty feet. I asked what type of shoe she wanted and she answered that she wanted a good comfortable work shoe. She gave me her work number and was told I would call when they were ready.

I was working on her shoes and Henry made the comment that I was putting most of the work on him because all of my attention was going into these new shoes. I chuckled and Henry told me that I must be sweet on her and I told him that I don't even know if she is single or married. I called Elizabeth and she came to the shop and she told me the shoes fit perfectly. She paid for them and left. I told Henry that I would probably never see her again. To my surprise she came back in two days. She asked if I could make a pair of shoes for a clubfoot. I told her of course I could because I had made several such shoes in Russia. She explained that Mr. Skelly had a clubfoot and couldn't find a shoemaker that made a shoe that didn't hurt. I told her to have Mr. Skelly come to my shop and I would measure his feet. To my surprise the next day a large black car pulled up in front of my shop. Out stepped Elizabeth with Mr. Skelly.

I never had met Mr. Skelly but I assumed it was him. We were introduced and he said that Elizabeth told him that I could make a shoe that didn't hurt his foot. I said I had made shoes for clubfeet in Russia and I would sure try. He said if I could do that I would be the only shoemaker that could. I took him into the back and measured his feet. I told him to come back in three days and he could try on the shoe. He and Elizabeth left and Henry said, if you get Mr. Skelly's business that I would be moving up. I told Henry that if I moved up he would move up with me and I also said I wanted to know more about Elizabeth.

I worked on that shoe for three days and those three days drug by very slowly. I had a rough shoe made and I called Mr. Skelly's office and told him to come by the shop. He came in his car but this time without Elizabeth. The shoe was rough but I wanted to get the correct shape before making the finished shoe. He put in on and stood up and said, "My God, this is the first shoe that hasn't hurt my foot." I felt around on the shoe, made a few finishing chalk marks, and told him in a few days it would be finished and I would call him. I then measured his other foot and he left.

It took one week but the shoes were finished. Henry told me that all the other work was backing up and I told him that if we get Mr. Skelly's business, I would hire another worker. Mr. Skelly came to the shop after I called him. He put on both shoes and walked around the shop. It was almost like watching a child with a new toy. He said that his feet had never felt so good. I told him that I could make a shoe that fit so well no one could tell he had a clubfoot. He told me his driver would bring all of his shoes over to make the same shoe to fit him. I asked how many pair. He said ten pair of shoes and four pair of boots. I told him to sit down because I wanted to measure his foot again to make a last impression in the shape of his foot if I was going to make that many pair.

I was measuring his foot when he mentioned Elizabeth and how she had told him I could make the shoe. I asked what her position was and he said she was a clerk in his office. He added that he thought she might be sweet on me. I almost dropped the tape and he said, "Looks like you might be sweet on her also." I told him that I was a Jew. He said, "What difference does that make, she is a nice young girl, a hard worker and you should ask her out."

I couldn't believe what I was hearing, this would never happen anywhere else but in America. To my surprise, the next day Mr. Skelly's driver came with all of the shoes and Elizabeth. They were carrying the shoes in and I was making notes and I asked Elizabeth if I could call on her. She blushed, looked down and said, "Yes." She told me there was to be a singing on Sunday at Swan Lake on the west side of Tulsa. Swan Lake was a pond fed by a spring and when I first came, it was a watering hole for cattle and horses. The city had grown and Swan Lake was now a park off Utica Avenue. Originally Swan Lake was called Orcutt Lake because it was on a ranch owned by Adolphus Orcutt. I was informed Mr. Orcutt was a Civil War veteran and had moved to this area in 1870 and began working in the cattle industry and found this spring-fed pond. I don't know when it started to be called Swan Lake.

I went to the Temple and told the Rabbi that I had met a very nice girl. He was pleased and asked what was her name. He assumed it was a girl from the community. I told him she was not a Jew and he said it would not work. I told him it would work if we wanted it to work. He told me that he had seen many of these marriages and they didn't work. I told him this one was different and he said that is what they all said.

Time dragged by very slowly and I went to pick up Elizabeth. She lived with three other girls in a house on South Boston. I met the three girls she lived with and we headed for Swan Lake. She had packed a picnic lunch and people were sitting on the grass around the pond. The singing group was from Hot Springs, Arkansas, and performed for people that came to the bathhouses and they came to Swan Lake on a regular basis. We were walking to claim our spot and we saw Mr. and Mrs. Skelly. They came over and I was introduced to Mrs. Skelly. Mr. Skelly walked

Orcutt Park Lake, Tulsa, Okla.

This is an old photo of Swan Lake or Orcutt Lake.

around and said, "You were right, no one can tell I have a clubfoot," He went on to tell that his foot had not felt so good in his whole life.

Elizabeth's parents were not too pleased that she was seeing a Jew, but we became engaged and were to be married in June of 1926. After we were engaged, I told Elizabeth and her parents about the farm at Boynton and the oil wells and they were not quit as unhappy. I made sure they didn't know about the money until after we were engaged. My clerk, Sarah, had married in 1923 and left the shop and Elizabeth said she would come to work. When Mr. Skelly found this out he told me he was losing one of his best employees but was happy for her. He also said she was the reason his feet felt so good because she found my shoe shop. We were married in the Temple and Solomon and his wife came from Dallas along with Uncle Herman and Aunt Rachel. It was a good ceremony and we had a good honeymoon also but I won't go into that. Elizabeth even converted to Judaism and this is what really brought me back to my faith.

The 1930s were not as good as the 1920s. The Great Depression hit and if not for the oil business, Tulsa would have been hit very hard. The price of oil did drop and a lot of people were out of work. I had hired another man in the shop but had to let him go when the Depression hit. Elizabeth and I made frequent trips to Boynton. We had started building a house and dreamed of the day we could finish it and have a home in the woods away from the city, but that would be a long time off now. I wanted to be a farmer and a rancher but didn't know enough to make a living and I couldn't be a shoemaker in the woods. I talked to the Rabbi saying I wanted to be a farmer and a shoemaker. He said it would be good to put the land into production but he told me I was a shoemaker, not a farmer.

I saw Mr. Laudaman downtown the next day. He was a member of the community and had a glass business in Tulsa. I repeated what the Rabbi had told me and he pointed across the street to a man and said, "That is Mr. Box and used to be a farmer but lost everything because of the Depression and in bad debt but he is a good man." I yelled at Mr. Box and told him to come across the street which he did.

Mr. Laudaman introduced us and I told him that I had a farm near Boynton and I wanted to put it back into production. The next day Henry and Elizabeth watched the shop and I took Mr. Box to Boynton. We walked the land and talked about what could be raised and he told me what breed of cattle would be best. I didn't know much about farming or ranching but he seemed to know what he was talking about. After about two hours I told him that I had made a decision. I wanted him to take the farm and we would split everything down the middle. If we had two calves, he would have one and I would have one. If we had twenty bushels of corn, he would have ten bushels and I would have ten bushels.

He looked at me in disbelief. "Are you serious?" he asked. I told him I had never been more serious in my life, but it would take a while to finish the house. He said that he and his three sons could finish the house. I told Elizabeth what I had done and she said that was an awful quick decision. I told her I wanted to put the land into production and it would also help Mr. Box. She asked how well I knew Mr. Box and I told her that if Mr. Laudaman thought he was a good man, he was all right.

The next morning, Mr. Box brought his wife and sons to the shop and Elizabeth and I met them. I could tell by the way they were dressed that times were hard. I asked if he could get workers to help with the house such as electricians and plumbers. He said that he knew a lot of good house builders that were out of work. I gave him the keys to my car and told him to get started. Elizabeth tugged at my arm and I patted her hand. Mr. Box then asked if he could move his family out to the farm. I told him the house wasn't finished then he said he couldn't afford to live in Tulsa anymore and could make out very well on the farm. I told him the first thing we needed to do was have a well drilled because there was no water on the farm. We shook hands and he took over the entire farm project. After he left Elizabeth said she had reservations but thought I had made a good decision.

In two and half months the well had been drilled and the house completed. The house was made of cement blocks and was well constructed. The best thing, everything was paid for. The Kerbel Farm was in operation. I went to the cattle sales with Mr. Box and he knew his cattle. He bought calves and raised them. If they looked good they were added to the herd. If they didn't look good to him they were sold. I was able to buy more land and now owned 320 acres. The Box family was also doing very well. Once a week he came by the shop and reported on how things were progressing. They had put in a three-acre truck garden and a two-acre watermelon patch. I never doubted his honesty. He kept excellent records and we shared equally in everything and I even learned about cattle from Mr. Box.

Elizabeth and I bought a new home. It wasn't new but was new to us. Mr. Box came by one Sunday afternoon and we had a good visit. His family had been on the farm almost four years now. We had lunch and as he was leaving he began talking. He said when I called his name that day on the street in Tulsa he was just walking around, not knowing how he was going to feed his family that day. He had been given food in soup lines and knew that couldn't last. He was convinced they would have starved to death because he had lost his farm and couldn't afford the rent on the apartment where they were living. He repeated that I saved his life and his family. I told him he was a good friend and was taking good care of the farm. As the years passed we became even closer friends.

The depression was getting deeper and the shoe business was very bad. People would come off the street and asked if they could have their shoes repaired but didn't have any money. They were putting cardboard or anything they could find to fill the holes in their shoes. I always repaired their shoes and told them to pay me when they were able. I never expected to be repaid by any of them but I thought back to the time when I had 75 cents in my pocket in Galveston and never turned anyone away. An Army man came in to put a heel back on his boot that had just fallen off. I told him he would have to wait just a minute. I was nailing a piece of leather on the bottom of a shoe for a man. I handed him the shoe and told him to pay me when he had the money and not to worry about it. The man in uniform asked if I did this often. The man whose shoe I had just repaired turned and said, "Mr. Kerbel is well known for fixing shoes and doesn't ask any money, but I will pay you when I can."

I told the man in uniform that it was my way of helping pay back what I owed this country. He said he was in charge of the Civilian Conservation Corps Camp located in the Osage Hills northwest of Tulsa. He said there were about 300 men in the camp and they had a shoe repair shop but couldn't keep up with the boots that were being worn out. They were building a new park in the Osage Hills between Pawhuska and Bartlesville. He said he would recommend my shop for the excess boot work from the camp. The next week a form came for me to fill out which I did with my bid but never expected to hear anything. In two weeks the man returned and said I had gotten the contract. Boots started coming in the next day and I began repairing about 100 pairs of boots each month and had to hire another man to help Henry.

The Temple set up a soup kitchen to help feed the people and I gave money on a regular basis. The Catholic Church also had a soup line and I gave them money and continued to repair shoes for people that needed it at no charge. But people began to come to the shop. I had repaired their shoes and they had found work and came back and paid me. I didn't know what to charge because I didn't know what I had done to their shoes so I only asked 25 cents and all that money went for the soup kitchens.

The business increased and I had a good positive cash flow. I had kept in contact with Mr. Cox from whom I had bought the land and thought it was ironic. I bought the land from Cox and Box was living there now. Three of the Cox children were attending Chilocco Indian School, which was near Ponca City. I asked why his children were attending a school so far from home? He explained that the school had been established in 1883 to "Anglicize" the children of the Plains Indians and now was a high school and taught various trades to the children. I asked who were the Plains Indians and he explained that the Plains Indians lived in the Great Plains were not part of the Five Civilized Tribes that had been brought from the southeastern part of the United States to Indian Territory in the 1830s on what was called the Trail of Tears. It was hard for me to understand the differentiation between the Civilized Indians and the Non-Civilized Indians.

I always felt I owed Mr. Cox something because of my good fortune. I thought for several months then told Mr. Cox that I wanted to visit the school because I had an idea. He was curious and I explained that I wanted to build a shoe shop at the school and he thought it was a good idea. The following Monday, Henry and Elizabeth manned the shop and I went on the train with Mr. Cox to Chilocco. The trip to Ponca City took about three hours and I saw an area of Oklahoma that was new to me. The Chilocco Indian School camp was well groomed and the stone buildings dated from the 1890s and early part of the 20th century. The school was a boarding school for Indian students. I met Mr. Correll, the Superintendent of the school and he was a very pleasant man. He assured Mr. Cox that his children were doing very well and I interrupted that was not the reason why we came. Because of my good fortune, I wanted to repay something to the Indian community. I explained my idea of the shoe shop at the school and he seemed intrigued. He said that he could probably find the money somewhere and I told him that I wanted to pay for the shop. I told him how I bought the land from Mr. Cox and then oil had been discovered and I wanted to pay back some of my good fortune. I told him that with his help we could find a young man to teach how to make a good boot and shoe and he could be the instructor.

We discussed the project for about an hour, then Mr. Correll took Mr. Cox and me on a tour of the school. It was well laid out. He explained that the school ran on a military plan and the students were assigned to companies. He also said that one of the main subjects was agricultural farming and animal husbandry for the boys and home economics for the girls. Mr. Cox met with his three children while Mr. Correll and I continued the tour. Most of the day was spent at Chilocco then we returned to Tulsa. We didn't talk much on the return trip but Mr. Cox did make a comment that I was a good friend to the Indians.

In two months, I received a letter from Mr. Correll. The project of the shoe shop had been approved. I immediately began a search for new equipment. I found what I wanted in Chicago and the day after I ordered the new machines, Mr. Evans came into my shop and gave me a check for $75.00 for the treadle machines I had given him. I told him the machines were a gift to help him get back on his feet but he insisted of paying for them. I told him that I didn't need the money and he explained that his shop was back into operation and he wanted to pay for the machines. He insisted and I told him I would use the money to help pay for the shop at Chilocco. He said it was a good project. He had known Henry for many years and they were talking about the Chilocco project. Mr. Evans said he had two grandsons that were attending Langston College. I had heard of Langston. It had been established in 1897 as the Oklahoma Colored Agriculture and Normal University and many young blacks from Tulsa went there. After Mr. Evans left Henry said a project like Chilocco would be good at Langston. His brother had sent his children there and it was a good school.

I decided to do the same project at Langston University. I contacted Mr. Evans and said I would like to visit Langston and would he help me. He contacted his grandsons who went to the office of the president, Mr. Isaac W. Young. Again Henry and Elizabeth manned the shop while I was off on another trip. Langston was just east of Guthrie, Oklahoma and Jim and I talked about the shoe business in Tulsa but the riot was not brought up. The pogrom in Odessa was painful to me and knew the riot was a painful topic for him. We met with Mr. Young and explained the project and what I was doing at Chilocco and he said he thought the idea would easily be approved. Langston was not like Chilocco. Chilocco was a boarding school for high school students but Langston was a university and the students lived in dormitories. Langston wasn't as regimented as Chilocco, after all Chilocco was planned on the military way of life.

I doubled my order from Chicago and ordered eight machines. I felt sorry for Henry and Elizabeth. I almost abandoned the shop. I was spending quite a few days at Chilocco getting the machines installed and the shop set up. A space in one of the big buildings had been set aside for the shoe shop and it was quite nice. The same thing at Langston, a space was found in the one of the buildings and all they needed were two men to run the shops. Mr. Correll introduced me to John Little Bear. He had attended Chilocco several years earlier and was told he was a good hard worker. Mr. Correll said he would be the best man to run the shoe shop. Of course he had no background in the shoe business so I brought him back to Tulsa. We found a small apartment where he was to stay and he became an apprentice in the shop.

Mr. Correll was right, John was a good worker and picked up the boot and shoe business very quickly. I was paying for everything to get him started because I felt this helped repay my good fortune. The next week, Bill Evans came to the shop. He was the son of Jim Evans and had attended Langston and Mr. Young agreed to pay for his apprenticeship in the shop. The next eighteen months were busy. I taught John and Bill everything I knew of making a good boot and shoe. Henry was a good teacher also. After all, he had been in the shoe business for many years. Between the two of us both John and Bill were ready to take over their respective shops. Those were good times and for the next two years, I made trips to Chilocco and Langston just to see how they were doing and they were graduating many good boot makers. I made many good friends at Chilocco and Langston through the shops.

Chapter Fifteen
The Rest is History

The 1930s were passing and letters became fewer and fewer from Mama and Gueti. I called them on the telephone one day their telephone didn't work anymore. I hadn't heard from Rosa in quite a while and I wrote Mama about this but she never answered my letter. I didn't know where Rosa was and what had happened to her. I was the oldest in the family and had the responsibility to take care of everyone. I wrote and called Solomon and told him that I wanted to go to Poland. He said that was impossible and Europe was on the brink of another war. He told me that he had been getting fewer letters from Mama and he didn't know what had happened to Rosa. They were still in Warsaw and the situation in Europe was not good.

Hitler had taken over as Chancellor of Germany and had taken over Austria. I read the news every day and wondered when someone was going to stand up to him. He had been rattling sabers for years and then his talk of the superiority of the Aryan Race was making news. I wasn't aware of the Aryan Race. I thought we just had one race, the human race. The last letter I got from Mama was in 1938. The next year Germany invaded Poland and the war began. I was going to Poland and bring Mama and Gueti to America and find out where Rosa was. There was talk in the Temple of the hatred Hitler and his henchmen had for the Jews, but this was nothing new. It seemed the world has hated the Jews for thousands of years. I wrote letters and tried to call but the telephones didn't work. I contacted the office of Senator Thomas, Governor Marland and even the Mayor of Tulsa, Mr. Penny. I got form letters from the office of Senator Thomas and Governor Marland thanking for me contacting their office. The mayor wrote that he had no dealings in international affairs.

Germany invaded Poland from the west on September 1st, 1939, and the Russians invaded from the east. The war had started. No one had stood up to Hitler and now he was running over Europe. I went to Dallas to visit Solomon and we agreed that we would never hear from Mama, Gueti or Rosa again. Then the Japanese bombed Hawaii and America was in the war. I was now a citizen but too old to serve. I was 53 years old. I bought thousands of dollars of bonds in the bond drives and I helped with the scrap metal drives. Elizabeth worked in the canteen at the station when the troop trains came through. America had come together to win the war. I was hoping we could win the war soon enough to save the rest of my family.

Rationing started and I made sure the shop was run according to the ration office. Most of the leather was going for the war effort and I couldn't make new boots and shoes if I wanted. I heard of a factory in Wichita, Kansas that was making leather flying suits for the Air Corps and there were other factories just like this one across the country. The whole community joined in. A lady come to the shop and said she was in charge of collecting bacon grease for the war effort. She chuckled when I told her that we were Jews and didn't eat bacon. She apologized and I told her she was doing a good job and we all had to work together to win the war.

In the early part of the war, we were losing. The Navy and most of the Air Corps had been destroyed in Hawaii and the Philippines. Then the Philippines fell and Japan was advancing. We had to defeat Japan but I wanted to know about Mama, Gueti and Rosa and the whole Jewish community in Europe. Mr. Box had two sons join the Army and Mr. Little Bear at Chilocco said many boys from Chilocco went to the service. He told me there was a National Guard Company at Chilocco and the whole unit went to war. Mr. Evans kept me informed of his family. He told me several boys from Langston had gone to Tuskegee Institute and became pilots in the Air Corps. I wanted to do more. I kept the shop open and the whole community was praying for all of our families.

The war dragged on and the tide changed. The battles of the Coral Sea and Midway stopped the Japanese and the Nazis were driven out of North Africa and then we invaded Sicily and Italy and finally Normandy. Then news of the death camps came. I knew these couldn't be true until the photographs came. I knew what had happened to Mama, Gueti, Rosa and everyone else I had known in Russia, Germany and Poland. I looked at the photographs of Auschwitz, Dachau and Buchenwald and knew everyone had suffered a horrible death at the hands of these Nazis. I knew my world was almost gone. Everyone I had known in Europe was dead. Six million Jews were dead and no one knows how many were dead to win this awful war. I was bitter. I wanted to hit back at someone. Elizabeth tried to comfort me and the only comfort I had was the visits Solomon made to me or I made to him.

Uncle Herman and Aunt Rachel had been dead several years and Solomon was the only family I had left. Then I realized I had the community in Tulsa. They were my family. We had memorial services for the dead and the people of Tulsa turned out. Word spread that my family had died in the Holocaust and people came by the shop. Strangers stopped me on the street and expressed sympathy. Elizabeth shared my grief. We had no children. It was not meant to be. The only thing I left of my family were three photographs that had been sent from Russia. Even Papa's and Simon's graves had been destroyed. My world was shaken down to its roots. I tried not to carry hatred in my heart, but the pogrom in Odessa, the riot in Tulsa and now the death camps in Europe consumed me. It was a pain that would not go away. My mother, sister, her husband and three children were all burned up in the concentration camps during the holocaust. Six million Jews were killed.

People have told me that Jews ran to the forest to hide and bounty hunters brought them in and were paid a dollar a person they brought in. How can people like this call themselves Christian? But that is a whole life time away and I still think of them but I am not bitter. I am too good a human being to be bitter.

I told Elizabeth that I wanted to start helping children. We started by donating money to the Temple that would be used to help Jewish children that were orphans because of the Holocaust. We also donated money to help people that had survived the Holocaust to find family members and get their lives back together. The state of Israel was established and Elizabeth and I donated money. The Jews now had a home. After Israel was established, the war started in the Holy Land. People that had been friends were now fighting each other. We heard of the people that had been uprooted and moved out to create Israel and I didn't know if this was right or not. It brought back memories of the family being uprooted and forced to leave Roshen. The whole world had been turned upside down by the war and would take generations to heal the wounds and I don't think many of the wounds would ever heal. Solomon and I tried and tried to find Mama, Gueti and Rosa but to no avail. I finally resigned myself that no one had survived.

Through the Temple we also began donating money to orphanages that had been established in Europe. These were set up for children who had lost both parents in the war. Elizabeth then suggested that we help orphans in the United States and Oklahoma. We gave money to the Temple and the Catholic Church to be used for children's projects. Children became an obsession with me. I set up a fund where I gave money to the children's ward at the three hospitals in Tulsa and the Children's Hospital in Oklahoma City. Children were the hope of the future. There was too much hatred in the world and children don't hate unless they are taught to hate.

The shop had a good business but Henry and I were getting old. In 1964, Mr. Box had made enough that he was able to purchase the farm. I was glad to sell this to him. I was too old to be a farmer now. I had good memories of the farm and all the work we had done together. Elizabeth and I visited the farm often and were always welcomed in their home. We often visited their home during Christmas and Mr. Box and his wife even came to Tulsa several times and helped light the Hanukkah candles.

Then in 1966 the rest of my world died. Elizabeth passed away. My reason for living was gone. Two months after her death, I took a trip with my two nephews to Israel and planted a tree in memory of the family. This was the only way I could keep them alive. I gave a window to the new Synagogue in Tel-Aviv. A new Synagogue was being built in Tulsa and I established a scholarship in memory of Elizabeth. The Star of David that was in the gable was removed and installed in the new building.

Henry died in 1970 and I sold the shop. Shoemakers were no longer in demand. It seemed people bought a new pair of boots or shoes instead of having the old ones repaired. The house was empty now and in 1976 I sold it and moved into an apartment at 15th and Peoria in Tulsa. This is when I met Sister Edith. She worked at St. John's Hospital and I went on a regular basis for checkups. I was introduced to her as the man who was giving money to the Children's Ward at the hospital. I was now 88 years old and we became good friends. She would stop by to say hello and check on me. She even helped me make out the checks for the children's groups that Elizabeth and I had donated money. Sister Edith would take me to the Temple and I'm sure some people thought this was a strange sight. Here was a Catholic nun bringing an old Jew to the Synagogue. She always came by and helped me light the candles for Hanukkah.

I made trips to Chilocco and Langston and visited the shoe shops. It always made me feel good when a student from Chilocco or Langston would stop by. It made me feel good that I was able to help in some small way.

I watched Tulsa grow and went to the Temple. Many friends came to visit but they were all getting older also and of course Mr. Box and his family always came to visit. They would always send me a Christmas gift and I always sent them a gift for Hanukkah.

I fell and broke a hip in 1984 when I was 96 years old. I had a hip replacement at St. John's Hospital and was able to get around but not like I used to. While I was in the hospital, Sister Edith was always at my bedside. I couldn't drive anymore and friends would come and take me on my errands and of course Sister Edith would take me places. Then Joe Todd came and did a series of interviews with me. He wanted to know about my childhood in Russia and it was strange to talk about these stories. We did these interviews over a three-year period. One of the most interesting times was when Sister Edith and Joe Todd took me to the Temple. Joe was in the Army Reserves and he came by one morning in uniform on Saturday morning. Sister Edith and me were just preparing to go to Temple and Joe came with us. Here I was an old Jew with a Catholic Nun and a young man who attended the Episcopal Church in Army uniform going to the Temple. I was very proud that day and I think we made quite a group that day. Everyone was so friendly and to Sister Edith and Mr. Todd and it made me even prouder.

Then came my 100th birthday party on December 15th 1988. It was held at my apartment and the Rabbi with many people from the Tempe and here along with Sister Edith and Father Halpin from the Catholic Church, Brother Reed from the Baptist Church and of course Mr. Box brought his family. Mr. Todd brought his mother and his uncle from Bartlesville. Several former students from Chilocco and Langston came by. Here was a cross section of society and that would not normally be found together. Farmers, Jews, Catholics, Baptists, Episcopalians, Native Americans and Blacks were all at my birthday party and I only wish Elizabeth could be here. She would have so much enjoyed this. I watched the people talk to each other and how each of them had met me, then we had birthday cake and they all sang Happy Birthday to me. We had a good time and then Mr. Box asked me to tell the story of the old country and how I came to America and how I ended up in Tulsa. I asked him to hand me Mama's Oil Lamp and I began telling the story of Mama and Papa and Roshen.

THE END

About Joe Todd

Since his notable service in the U.S. Army and employment at the Oklahoma Historical Society, retired Major Joe L. Todd has been a volunteer for the Dwight D. Eisenhower Library interviewing World War II veterans, conducting to date over 2,300 interviews which have been archived in various libraries and museums.

Major Todd has also authored two other book titles, *USS Oklahoma, Remembrance of a Great Lady*, published in 1990 by Taylor Publications, and *Robert Huston, Oklahoma Rough Rider*, published in 1998 by the Oklahoma Historical Society, helping to tell the story of military service.

He regularly speaks at meetings, appears on television and radio, and authors a newspaper column and stories relating the exploits of Oklahoma veterans.

In 2007 he received the Oklahoma Heritage Association Award for his weekly column of stories about Oklahomans' service during World War II published in the Bartlesville Examiner-Enterprise.

An active Oklahoma Military Hall of Fame Ambassador, he has established a scholarship through the Oklahoma Historical Society to recognize young students who interview Oklahoma veterans.

His impressive and innovative service to Oklahoma Veterans has spanned three decades and continues without pause.

Made in the USA
Coppell, TX
06 May 2021